Indian Writing Today

In the same series

Indian English Literature since Independence
K. Ayyappa Paniker

Indian Writing Today

Essays in honour of

Professor L.S.R. Krishna Sastry

Edited by

C. R. Visweswara Rao

IAES

Indian Association for English Studies

Published by
Indian Association for English Studies
c/o J 391, New Rajinder Nagar,
New Delhi 110 060
in association with
Intellectual Book Corner
New Delhi

1996

Photo Typesetting by
Pivot Computers
Delhi 110 006

Printed at
Mehra Offset Press
New Delhi 110 002

Contents

Poetry

Drama

Fiction

Preface

The late Professor L.S.R. Krishna Sastry was elected Vice-President of the Indian Association for English Studies in 1992 at the 40th All India English Teachers' Conference held at Sri Krishnadevaraya University, Anantapur. His long and outstanding services to the cause of English studies in India were thus recognized. Starting his research under the supervision of Professor K.R. Srinivasa Iyengar on Sir William Jones, Professor Krishna Sastry diversified his interests in due course and came to be known for his especial fascination for Indian literature in English. Also, he was fond of Indian classical music and his occasional column in *The Hindu* offered a fine critique of today's classical music. This collection of essays, *Indian Writing Today*, is brought out in his honour as a scholarly tribute to his teaching and research in this area. Professor Sudhakar Pandey and Dr. R.K. Dhawan endorsed this mode of honouring the late Professor L.S.R.K. and I owe them a deep debt of gratitude.

We are so deeply entrenched in contemporary reality that it is not easy for us to locate a vantage point from where to offer an assessment of our literature or make pronouncements or predictions that guide us to contemporary writing. Apart from the "big three," Mulk Raj Anand (with his theme of "the poetry is in the pity"), R.K. Narayan (with his imaginary homeland Malgudi which symbolizes India with its rootedness of culture and its current tensions and traumas and perplexities and points of view), and Raja Rao (with his metaphysical quest for a re-discovery of an ancient, not antiquated, rhythm in contemporary life), all of whom have continued to be productive in the 1980s and 1990s, Nayantara Sahgal, Anita Desai, Manohar Malgonkar, Arun Joshi, Khushwant Singh, Shashi Deshpande have exploited the radical challenges India is facing in its sociological landscape as well as in the immemorial landscape of its heart so as to give expression to the clash between the mores of a pre-urban civilization and those of the industrialized, pseudo-westernized society. Some of these artists have dwelt upon Gandhian values and the contemporary retreat from them in order to give images of a society in throes of change and facing the onslaught of the pre-colonial mentality in the post-colonial context. There are other writers, some born in the 1930s and 1940s and some born in the 1950s and 1960s, whose contribution, bewilderingly wide-ranging, gives us a taste of the heterogeneity of the cultural space we inhabit. These include Ranga Rao, Gopal Gandhi, Vijay Singh, Partap Sharma, Vikram Seth, Amitav Ghosh, Shashi Tharoor, J. Allan Sealy, Upamanyu Chatterjee, Gita Mehta, and so on. If, in addition, we take writers of Indian origin into consideration, with V.S. Naipaul, Salman Rushdie, and Bharati Mukherjee who have had phenomenal success, we have a plenitude of writing, and the literary scene seems to quicken with renewed life. In the field of poetry, A.K. Ramanujan, R. Parthasarathy and others have opened up possibilities of an unchaining of the English chains and introduced a bi-literary strain. Vikram Seth's experiment, poem into novel, foreshadows the discovery of literary forms in tune with the post-modern movement in literature.

The post-*Midnight's Children* phase, with its innovative fictional techniques replacing the earlier realistic strain, seems to offer new possibilities. Shashi Tharoor's *The Great Indian Novel*, for example, places before us the saga of Indian history mixing fact and fiction, myth and history, and epic and mock-heroic in a panoramic allegory. It is an attempt to re-tell the political history of twentieth century India through a fictionalized recasting of events and episodes of the ancient epic. In an exciting period of a re-drawing of the literary map of India as it were, Rushdie attempts to grasp the elusive, multi-dimensional truth of India's social and political milieu by the technique of magical realism in which history, myth, allegory, mock-epic, autobiography, dream, fantasy—rather every technique traditional or modern—are welded in order to dislocate language into meaning and thus present the complex image of post-Independence India. Amitav Ghosh's *Shadow Lines* with its lyrical prose, complex time-frame and the protagonist's simultaneous perception of differing levels of reality, and Upamanyu Chatterjee's *English August: An Indian Story* with its dramatization of the realities of everyday regional and ethnic life with relentless objectivity are part of the mosaic. And there are Mukul Kesavan's *Looking through Glass*—a characteristically post-modern novel—which reveals through its treatment of history a concern with magical realism held out as a proper form for the Indian novel and Gita Mehta's *A River Sutra* which intertwines the ancient and the modern as seen through its foregrounding and framing revealing a *sutra* in the transactions of the human race as exemplified by the river Narmada. With its multiple narratives and incorporation of a variety of genres, *A River Sutra* is a subversive post-modern text illustrating yet another kind of being "handcuffed to history." These various modes of representing fictional landscapes and mirroring life's complexities show the contemporary Indian novel coming to terms with India's legacy and the post-colonial ambience.

C.R. VISWESWARA RAO

In Memoriam

Professor L.S.R. Krishna Sastry

T. RAMESH DUTTA

Professor Sastry is no more. This is a sad day for us all in the English Department of the Andhra University. The social, cultural, and spiritual life of Visakhapatnam will never be the same again. As a montage of memories cascades across the mind's eye flashing bits and pieces from four decades, since the English (Hons.) days of 1955, I recognize the brilliant student, the dedicated researcher, the committed teacher which he had always been. Well, we had our differences as who had not, but Sastry would invariably come up with the playful pun and proverb, and have his way, not scoring a point, but winning you over.

If there was a PR man better than professional, it was Sastry. His amazingly facile range of style and address endeared him to people from all walks of life—officials and laymen, artists and critics, students and colleagues. He was an Organization Man too, unruffled by upsets, ever ready with impromptu adjustments, comfortable himself, no less comforting to others. He proved again and again that making friends is an art, and keeping them a fine art.

Attuned to the cherished values of our tradition, Sastry took upon himself the propagation of our culture and heritage through professional service and informal channels. For all his modernity, erudition and sophistication, his presentations were simple, sincere and forthright, with a characteristic flair for rhythm, melody and harmony. Few who have heard him can forget the modulations and pauses of his voice. A speaker, widely known and respected, Sastry always carried his audiences beyond the hour and the agenda, for such is his magnetism.

Traditions did not make Sastry hide-bound or sour-faced. His was an equable temper. With a critic's eye for talent, and an amateur's joy in beauty, he was ever the connoisseur of the fine arts. At the many concerts and dance recitals in and around Vizag, his introduction was never conventional, his thanksgiving never ritualistic. The maestro and the

Courtesy: A.I.R. Visakhapatnam

novice were greeted with equal courtesy and grace and the audience found themselves transported to a rich aesthetic experience.

I recall vividly Sastry, the English (Hons.) student, sitting in the front row and nodding his head during Prof. Srinivasa Iyengar's lectures on Shakespeare. Over the years Sastry made a mark in English Studies here and abroad. As an office bearer of the All India English Teachers' Association and of the Indian Association for Commonwealth Studies, he did commendable work. Though his primary interest lay in Indian English literature, he took considerable initiative in diversifying English Studies at the Andhra University. It is a pity that his promising career has been cut short before his dream of introducing Australian and Canadian literatures was fully realized.

Neither a cynic nor a fanatic, Sastry as 'LSRK' played a key role in the World Teacher Trust, the Sri Aurobindo Society, the Kala Bharati, and the Satya Sai Seva Organization, to name a few. The pace of death is inevitable even as it is irrevocable. But to have left behind a community of grateful students and a circle of warm friends and admirers is not given to everybody. To die in harness is the privilege of the chosen.

May his soul rest in peace.

Some Indic Views of Texts

M. SIVARAMAKRISHNA

One of the remarkale features of Indic views on texts is identifying them in terms of desire and fulfilment. These two: the urge for fulfilment and impulse behind that urge mark speculations on the nature of texts. In classical conceptions, we have as one of the components what is called *phalasruti,* the listening to the benefits accruing from reading a text. (Reading could also mean recitation and contemplation.) Therefore, we have the two major metaphors of *kamadhenu* and *kalpataru*, respectively, the cow of plenty and the tree of limitless fulfilment. The fact that *kama* represents one of the *purus'harthas—dharma, artha, moksha* being the other components—it is only legitimate that textual reading should be regarded as vitally linked with total fulfilment. It would, thus, include the apparently dichotomous *abhyudaya* and *nishreyasa,* the profane and the sacred. Similarly, *kalpa* could be linked to *sankalpa*, rightly motivated desire. Thus, texts are not exercises in cerebration but vitally linked to desire, and *kalpa*, the thought behind desire. To regard texts as *kamadhenu* and *kalpataru* is something unique to Indic views.

Basic to any understanding of the implications is appropriating the structure of orality. Most of the texts, specially the Vedic texts, were transmitted through generations with amazing concern for phonetic exactitude and rhythmic notations. From this orality stem the earliest speculations on the nature of the word, correct accent and exact meaning. Thus, we have the two-tiered structure of *sravana* and *manana*. One not only hears but listens and this listening is in terms of one's own reception mediated by the commentary, *vyakhyana*, given by the preceptor.

Before the other facets of this oral tradition are identified we have also to note that Indic texts assigned crucial significance to the testimony of word itself as revelation of truth, as one of the criteria of logical validity. This is called *sabda-pramana,* verbal testimony. If this appears too facile, only the words of a person who has the competence to speak becomes verbal testimony. *Sabda* becomes *pramana* when it is the *vakya* of an *apta,* an *aptavakya.* An *apta* is not someone who distorts words in an attempt to deceive and "sell" (our advertiser's copywriting is a remarkable instance of this) but one who possesses at least three virtues: s/he should be in a position to command or instruct by virtue of his/her ethically impeccable life; has realized/perceived *dharma,* the principle which sustains all our activities; has the disinterested desire to communicate the truth as a mode of liberation. Only then *sabda-pramana* rises to the level of *aptavakya.*

Thus conceived, orality implies several of our contemporary concerns. One cannot communicate even orally without a syntax. We have here the origins of grammar. Significantly enough, *vyakarana* or grammar, is accorded supreme primacy in any process of communication. Indeed, as one commentator puts it, grammar is the supreme science, the purifier of all sciences, the royal road free of all detours which aims at realizing one's supreme object. (One wishes that such a sacred view of grammar animates teachers of English grammar, morosely and mechanically going about drilling the "disinterested" student in subject-object-predicate, etc.) Grammar also involves ordinals/numbers. This has its roots in the sequentially structured elaborate rituals. They enact in a dramatic way what the sentence organizes in sequence. The one is physical, the verbal counterpart of which is grammar. Since grammar is not a mere succession of sounds, one has to make sense of what is heard. Here are the origins of textual interpretations which include very sophisticated views of meaning and significance.

Orality has further implications chief of which is *apaurusheya*. This is, approximately, anonymous text but universal truths revealed and then transcribed. That a text has no author except truths which it proclaims has great immediacy in the contemporary debate about the death of the author. One way to understand it would be to think of the reader as constituting the text. Moreover, if the presence of the author symbolizes the process of individuation, this egotistic sublime can be negated by making the text autonomous. Texts would then be available for endless deconstruction. The author as an individual signification has controversial dimensions, both positive and negative. It is in this context that one has to place the concept of *apaurusheya* as a tool of practical appropriation of texts. Even the most secular reading of a "sacred" text is validated by this kind of strategy of deauthoring a text. (One may argue that this reading of *apaurusheya* is far from what the classical views assume, but, then, all these concepts need appropriation in terms of contemporary idiom, an engagement which is hardly evident in the classically-oriented scholars).

Orality would also extend itself to what one can call the cumulative nature of commentary, which is one of the most remarkable features of

Indic interpretive traditions. The function of orally transmitting is not that of one expert parrot mouthing the same tunes and passing them on to the uninitiated fledglings. This is a very poor conception of what the idea of *sruti* implies. Each text as it was received was not only received but recast. For instance, Vedic commentaries by different sages provide intertexts of intricate significance. Similarly, if we take the *sutra* tradition Jaimini's *Mimamsa-sutras* are commented on by Sabara and Sabara's is further extended and often controverted by Kumarilabhatta. Analogously, on Panini's *Ashtadhyayi* there is Katyayana's *Vartika* (third century b.c.) and on both these Patanjali's *Mahabhashya* right up to Nageshabhatta in the late eighteenth and early nineteenth centuries.

Besides this feature the cumulative tradition also involves the functions of updating a text as well as transmitting the given one. Moreover, one of the consequences of this updating is redefinitions of key words. We notice not only categorization but alongside words defined from the perspectives of different disciplines. Thus, discipline-specific categories and their nomenclature are exempt from monolithic definitions. For example, the word *dravya* is a key word used with different, often contradictory, connotations.

II

Against this background, there are several structures or texts with amazingly clear-cut distinctions. Author-wise, for instance, we have at least five categories of texts: (a) texts based on *drastas* or texts which are revelations or, rather, verbalizations of truths seen in a transcendental state; (b) *prokta*—these are texts in which the composer is one but the expositor or teacher explicating the text is another. For example, the *Brahmanas;* (c) *upajnata*—these texts constitute truths or principles discovered and formalized by some one author. A classic example is Panini's *Mahabhashya;* (d) *krita*—these are ordinary texts originating from a specific author. Under this category we get poetry and other creative forms of writing. *Vyakhyana* or text as commentary is also identified as an autonomous structure. (One is tempted to think of this as the rudimentary form of "theory".)

This author-based categorization is only one facet of textual speculations. The more important thing is to identify stable categories which sustain redefinitions in the light of our present situation exemplifying an incredible range of criticism and theory. From this perspective four basic textual forms seem to me capable of fresh insights. These can be regarded—if such a thing is necessary—as indigenous analogues to our current assumptions about texts. Here one notices an identity between form and orientation. In other words, these are both texts and orientations, ideology as well as structure.

In these terms, the four basic textual categories are: *sruti, smriti, sastra, kavya.* Of these, with the hinterland of thought which we have now, *sruti* need not be identified as wholly religious texts. Since the Vedic texts abound in myth, symbol, philosophy and religion, the corresponding approach of the *sruti* is something which stems from all these concerns. Thus, our reading of a literary text in terms of its philosophical and religious implications is reading it in terms of the orientations that the *sruti* text traditionally sustained. *Sruti* thus is philosophic and religious implications inhering in a text. Since the Vedic texts are replete with far-ranging symbolic meanings this could also involve a close look at the symbols and metaphors marking a text.

The next category, *smriti*, is traditionally associated with the changing dialectics of social and related familial conventions. For example, *Manusmriti* is a compendium of principles that should regulate individual and interpersonal life. Since this involves the four major concerns of life—money, sexual gratification, controlled by ethics and freedom—*smriti* is a dynamic category which prevents the hardening of *sruti* into alleged eternal values. Therefore, texts are to be read in terms of values *(sruti)* but values which have to be constantly checked by contingent reality. In other words, if ideology is important, this ideology need not always be transcendental or foundational. A constant tension is thus capable of being traced in any text: the tension between what we identify today as the freedom to think and the constricted arena to act. Thus conceived, *sruti* and *smriti* are not fossilized texts irrationally inherited but mutually correcting approaches and orientations.

We now come to the basically discursive form called *sastra.* If we take the clue from the classic *Arthasastra* by Kautilya it is possible to identify these texts as specifically concerned with problems of civic life and its controlling conventions as identified in *dharmasastras*. Questions of a political nature are those which cannot be discussed in symbolic or metaphoric way. These require constant and clear formulations. This would therefore mean an approach based on the corresponding textual strategies of both constructing and criticizing. *Sastra* is not a specific text alone but a way of reading texts. One can mention the categories of *sastrapaddhati:* the *sastra* way of reading texts. This is a cluster of four items: (a) the formal organization of a text in terms of chapter, expository techniques, etc.; (b) the logical mode of advancing and sustaining an argument or the coherence (or its absence in creative texts) of what is said; (c) *pramanas* or the epistemological bases with assumptions about valid sources of knowledge, evidence provided, etc.;

(d) strategies or instruments of interpretation which stem from the nature of technical words used and their contextual meaning, etc.

Finally, we have the text called *kavya,* the imaginative construct. These are to be judged obviously in terms of formalistic, aesthetic approaches. Analysis of language and its role in such contexts is a sustained and elaborate (often over-elaborate) feature of Indic views. Ranging from *sphota* theory to *rasadhvani, kavya* is the residue of literary flavour which can be identified in any text.

III

So far we have considered *sruti, smriti, sastra, kavya* as various orientations governing the text as well as readings of the text. The "traditional" approaches such as the philosophic, the sociological, the linguistic and literary, and the formalistic are, to take the Western ambience, approximations to the fluid texts of *sruti, smriti, sastra, kavya.*

Another related concern is specific modes of interpretation. One can only have a cursory glance at the rich potential embedded in Indic views. Basically, several modes of interpretation are necessitated by the extremely cryptic/aphoristic nature of the text. Thus the *sutra* form has given rise to striking ways of possessing the text. These tools of taming the text have potential for being used to texts coming from even an "alien" ethos or, as the sacred cow of postmodernism would put it, the other. If *sutra* is the kernel, the barest thread without a single bead of elaboration, we have several ways in which it is subjected to explication. To begin with, we have *vritti* a commentary form specifically focussing on explication of the ideational element of a *sutra* corresponding roughly to thematics. An analysis of *vritti* itself, in turn, is called *paddhati.*

Subsuming these two, there is *bhashya*, a detailed analysis of the intentions, ends, arguments and counterarguments of a text. This process is extended by *samiksha* which is an explanation of the deeper suggested meanings and issues imbedded in the *bhashya.* The next process called *tika* is, roughly, grappling with the linguistic problems of a text. This is an attempt to express meaning in the simplest, briefest possible language. No elaborate and extended commentary is intended here. Some of the unfamiliar, archaic words are explained for, possibly, a new set of readers. Words which are evidently difficult either because of remoteness or pedantry are explained in an interpretative mode called *panjika.* From language to meaning we have the transition in a structure called *karika* which is a statement of the meaning of a *sutra.* (Guadapada's *Karika* on the *Mandukya Upanishad* is a representative example.) Finally, an analysis of the unexpressed and suggested implication called *var-*

tika rounds off this spectrum of Indic textual interpretative strategies. It is also necessary to underline the fact that these are not isolated autonomous units but an intricately intertwined cumulative cluster of interpretations.

IV

For determining the purport of a text also we have many ways of interpretation or giving form to our responses. For instance, we have a structure consisting of six determinative components. The first is called *upakramaupasamhara aikya:* this is explicating the unity of theme generally evident in the opening and closing passages of any text. The next step is to take account of the emphasis laid on crucial ideas/passages/words. This is called *abyasa.* The concept of repetition is not an inane attempt to mask poverty of thought but a rhetorical way of locating the controlling centres of a text. Repetition is also one way to neutralize resistance to new ideas. Eventually it achieves its culmination in *mantra* that which repeatedly contemplated upon leads us to freedom from the text and entry into its extension in life.

Repetition is an initial step to what is certainly central to the reading of texts: identifying the core of uniqueness which appropriated properly constitutes tradition. This is based on the assumption that all significant writing has the quality of not being available elsewhere in any other text. This is what is called *apurvata,* that which has no precedents. Then we have another step called *arthavada* or, roughly, interpreting passages of a polemical nature carefully. Passages of eulogy or acceptance of tradition without questioning and an irrational censure of tradition are some of the concerns of *arthavada.* The penultimate step is called *upapatti,* the evaluating or the logical consistency of any text. Finally, the most pragmatic test is applied: the benefits, both secular and sacred, accruing from the reading of/interpreting a text. This is *phala,* fruit, a tangible image of concrete gain.

V

This brief review should legitimately be rounded off by a glance at the linguistic speculations of the Hindus, which Julia Kristeva calls "the most ancient basis of modern abstract thought on linguistics." In the contemporary context of language as the construct of reality evident in the work of Nietzsche (problematic relation of language to reality), Pierce (semiotics; all human thought communicated in signs), Saussure (the arbitrary relation between the signifier and the signified), Wittgenstein (linguistic structuring of human experience as games people play), Heidegger (existentialistic critique of metaphysics), Sapir/Whorf (language shapes reality and is shaped by it), Foucault (genealogical quest for the social construction of knowledge) and above all Derrida (deconstructing any secure meaning in the text), the Indic views of language have their own potential.

For instance, the problem of constituting meaning is central to Hindu speculations. We have several schools which range from definitions of sentences to sophisticated analyses of meanings. It is interesting that even the definition of a sentence, as in the case of Katyayana, is rooted in the idea of desire. A sentence, he says, is "Something which has no requirement or expectation of words outside itself to complete its meaning." Expectation is a very bald translation of *nirakanksha* which once the negative is removed becomes desire or expectancy (what a contrast to the repetitive inanities of defining sentence as a group of words that makes sense! All the more funny since the word 'sense' is question-begging!)

Bhartrihari himself identifies a sentence in terms of humanly experienced *gunas: aikyata, yogyata* (compatability), *sanghata* (unity), *krama* (sequence), *samnidhi* (words should be contiguous in time), etc. Similarly words and their meanings are identified as *abhidha* (primary) *lakshana* (transferred), *vyanjana* (other than the literal or stated meaning). In effect, *shabda, rupa, artha, vyakarana* and *shrota* (name or sound, form, meaning, syntax, speaker/listener) together constitute different components of meaning-generation. The apex of this kind of speculation (speculation is *darshana*—seeing) is the *Sphota* theory with its different levels of comprehension such as *para, pasyanti, madhyama, vaikhari* which functioning together burst forth or bloom into understanding.

Finally, Indic views have important implications for *anuvada,* translations. If we assume, with Steiner, understanding itself as a process of translation, the Indic view of experience as beyond words rescues us from the anxiety to remain loyal to the "original." Since the transcendental signified is negated, any text in any language has no mimetic check of its meaning. Therefore, translations of Indic texts, particularly literary texts, need not be subjected to the eminently negatable process of checking their authenticity in terms of the original. Moreover, with Sanskrit remaining, for most people, a remote language the only text of Indic interpretations is the texts we have or we have to make in English. The different versions of the same text available in several Indian languages and their performative circumstances as in the case of the *Ramayana,* for instance, have interesting analogical implications for constituting Indic interpretative texts in English.

Psychoanalysis and Indian Writing in English: Promises and Possibilites

M. RAJESHWAR

Sigmund Freud, the father of psychoanalysis, acknowledged that poets and philosophers discovered the unconscious long before he did. For that reason he advised aspiring analysts to study literature as part of their training. Meredith Anne Skura goes a step further and argues: "the poets have discovered" not just the unconscious but "*psychoanalysis* before Freud did, and that at its subtlest and most wideranging. . . . It is not the mere presence or expression of primitive and unconsciously apprehended elements but the attempt to come to terms with them and to work them into the texture of conscious experience that makes the poets the predecessors of Freud."[1] Peter Brooks views the literary critic's job too to be not very different from that of the psychoanalyst: "I believe that the persistence in literary study must ultimately derive from the conviction that the materials on which psychoanalysts and literary critics exercise their powers of analysis are in some basic sense the same: that the structure of literature *is* in some sense the structure of mind."[2]

Indeed psychoanalysis and literature have always been viewed as two very closely related intellectual disciplines. Literature also provided a contiguous field of verification for psychoanalytical propositions. Freud was only too willing to borrow literary examples to prove analytical points. It is therefore not surprising that in the second half of this century psychoanalysis has emerged as a valid tool of literary criticism and gained wide acceptability among the critical and intellectual circles.

At present four widely practised psychoanalytic critical models are available. They base themselves on (a) the author and his unconscious sources (b) the putative unconscious of the literary characters (c) the unconscious response of the reader to the text and (d) the formal construction of the literary work focusing on its textual and rhetorical aspects. Apart from these, other models such as the "transferential model" (Peter Brooks), "dream-work model" (Terry Eagleton) and "the psychoanalytic process model" (Meredith Anne Skura) are also suggested. Each model is effective depending on the object of attention and the critic's purpose.

What distinguishes psychoanalytic literary criticism from other approaches is that it usually takes into account those aspects of the works which have been thought of as unimportant by the conventional critics. Its practice of integrating these very "messy details"[3] into serious discourse has enabled it to come out with new interpretations of literary works. Through the pioneering efforts of scholars such as Shoshama Felman, Irvin Malin, Jean Baker Miller, Shlomith Rimmon-Kenan etc., world classics had been brought under the psychoanalytic microscope and their continuing appeal was explained in scientific and psychological terms.

It is however disappointing to note that unlike the sociological approaches, which became popular with Indian critics with a surprising speed psychoanalysis, in spite of its obvious relevance to India, has made little or no impact on Indian criticism in English. Except some stray studies such as the ones by Usha Bande, Darshan Singh Maini and R.S. Sharma, no notable use of psychoanalytic concepts has been made in India to study our English literary works. Indian Writing in English seems to be in particular need of a new approach such as psychoanalysis for it certainly promises to earn it new respectability and wider acceptability on the world literary stage.

In this paper therefore I venture to suggest the possibility of making a fruitful use of psychoanalysis, especially psychoanalytic character study, for both creative and critical purposes and then argue that much of value would emerge from such endeavour.

As the noted Indian English novelist, Nayantara Sahgal, puts it "Fiction [and certainly Indian fiction in English] is about people, basically about character . . . a novel is concerned with the characters it creates."[4] The characters in Indian fiction are shaped after the Indian personality structure which is extremely complex and has eluded all categorization until it has been studied from the psychoanalytic angle. Therefore it becomes imperative both for the novelists and critics to understand this personality structure so as to authentically portray a character or to scientifically analyze it.

The Indian equivalent of the *id,* says Sudhir Kakar, is formed of a combination of the *chitta* and the *guna* constellation. *Id* is not viewed as a seething cauldron of instinctual drives but as aiming at 'altruism' and moving toward the realization of the purpose of human life. The newborn is believed to carry with him the three basic *gunas: sattva, rajas* and *tamas*. And if, in later life, *rajas* happens to be the dominant drive the individual has to expend large amounts of psychic energy to keep it in check for its free-pay amounts to practising *adharma.*

Indians have a "passive and less differentiated" ego in contrast with the "synthesizing and integrating activity" attributed to it in the West. In the Hindu scheme of things ego-reality (expressed in the West in terms of various ego functions such as a sense of reality, reality testing and adaptation to the environment) is of marginal importance. The whole of worldly experience is treated as a cosmic unreality. As against the classical psychoanalytic view of reality as tragic and ironic, the Hindu (more precisely the yogic) vision of reality is a

> combination of the tragic and the romantic. Man is still buffeted by fate's vagaries and tragedy is still the warp and woof of life. But instead of ironic acceptance, the yogic vision offers a romantic quest. The new journey is a search and the seeker if he withstands all the perils of the road, will be rewarded by an exaltation beyond normal human experience.[5]

Super-ego too seems to be weakly differentiated and insufficiently idealized in Indians. The tenets of *dharma,* the system of ideals, do not firmly entrench themselves in the individual's psychic structure but exist deep within, in close association with the other two sub-systems of personality. Whereas in the West an individual's behaviour is constantly regulated by the proscriptions of the *super-ego,* in a Hindu, it is regulated by what Sudhir Kakar calls "communal conscience." He explains that communal conscience which comprises family and *jati* norms "is a social rather than an individual formation: it is not 'inside' the psyche. In other words, instead of having one internal 'sentinel' an Indian relies on many external 'watchmen' to patrol his activities and especially his relationships in all the social hierarchies."[6] This creates a situation in which clandestine infringement of moral standards is a thing not to be much worried about.

The above analysis of the Hindu personality structure in psychoanalytic terms gives one clear insight into certain commonly observable traits, and external manifestations of behaviour.[7] Most Indians are at least in theory religious in outlook. An unshakable belief in the rebirth theory seems to have given them a leisurely attitude toward everything. They do not easily get disturbed over delays and failures nor do they mind postponing things without much regret. Life is viewed as a continuum traceable to several births before and extendible to several births after the present one. As a natural result, the Indian concept of time defies all attempts of definition in the Western philosophical terms. The Indian concept of time seems to have historical origins too. Ancient India experienced long periods of peace and prosperity. People lived mostly in the open, in benevolent geographical surroundings enjoying nature's bounty in an easy and relaxed atmosphere. This, coupled with the joint family system and a weakly differentiated *super-ego* have integrated into the Indian personality ready hospitality, sharing attitude, love for peace, aversion for aggressiveness and tolerance for the expression of ambivalence especially when it is not detrimental to 'communal conscience.' An off-shoot of the religious outlook is fatalism which appears to have given the Indians the ego-strength to maintain equanimity even in the face of unpleasant happenings. But at the same time the low achievement motivation is also often attributed to this trait. While the high premium the Westerners place on the tension between the ego and the *super-ego* results in guilt feelings which are ultimately channelized into a 'high potential for activity' an Indian is not induced into action by a strongly internalized agency. He can sit idly for hours and feel none the worse for it.

In their dealings with others, Indians often exhibit a strange admixture of inhibition and compromise on the one hand and communicative and intruding attitude on the other. The authoritarian joint family relations which made Indians depend on external authority figures to an excessive degree and the long periods of foreign domination account for the former and a readily accommodating nature and the basic trust in others may account for the latter. But surprisingly enough, centuries of subjugation has given them an unusual ability to survive through difficult times. Even in the face of oppressive and provocative circumstances Indians usually exhibit a forbearance rarely found elsewhere in the world.

On the negative side, Indians relatively lack integrity and honesty. The basic religious values of truth and honesty are rarely practised. Sincerity and direct statement of facts is generally disapproved of. The joint family atmosphere and the *jati* bonds have such profound influence on the individual that he begins to regard corruption, nepotism and dishonesty as mere abstract concepts. Immorality and illegality are irrelevant as long as one's acts do not vary from the "principle of primacy of relationships."

Dignity of labour is conspicuously absent in Indian society, especially among the people of middle-class origin who are incidentally the protagonists of most of the Indian novels. The almost uncritical preference for jobs of a certain kind and open dislike for labour intensive occupations has much to do with the traditional *varnavyavasta* which sought to sharply divide people on the basis of their vocations that enjoyed various degrees of respect and prestige. Another manifestation of the caste-system is status consciousness generally found in public life but more pronounced in family life where elderly and male members invariably enjoy greater respect than others.

The foregoing theoretical understanding of Indian psyche will surely offer fresh insights into and brighten the dark corners of especially the novels which lend themselves to psychoanalytic interpretation. One often notes that the protagonists of such novels deviate from these common Indian norms and therefore their life becomes worthy of narration. Anita Desai, Arun Joshi, Bharati Mukherjee and Nergis Dalal of the second generation Indian English novelists have portrayed, often with full knowledge of the tenets of psychoanalysis, literary personages in their moments of intense psychic struggle. The works of these writers are unamenable to conventional critical approaches. The sensitively portrayed characters of these novels are best appreciated critically in the light of the formulations of depth psychology.

However the Indian literary critic using the psychoanalytic formulations for critical purpose should do so with full knowledge of the fact that traditional psychoanalysis as it obtains in the West is not entirely applicable to the somewhat special literary and cultural environment of India. The Americans and the British too felt similarly and that is perhaps why native varieties of psychoanalysis such as Ego-psychology and Object Relations Theory have developed there and have been promptly assimilated by literary criticism.

Indians continue to be governed by group or *jati* norms. In other words, Indian society has not yet become an individualistic society. People are still viewed in relation to society rather than as separate entities in India. Therefore while the sociologically oriented later, Freudian 'Metapsychology' continues to be relevant to the Indian conditions. It should be further qualified by the findings and theories of Sudhir Kakar, Erik Erikson and Erich Fromm because they have added a psycho-social dimension to psychoanalysis. Sudhir Kakar has transplanted psychoanalysis on the Indian soil. He discussed psychology of Indians in terms of their myths, literature and popular culture in such of his works as *The Inner World, Shamans, Mystics and Doctors* and *Intimate Relations.* His contribution to the discovery of Indian personality structure in psychoanalytic terms has already been discussed earlier in this paper. Erikson's most significant contribution lies in the field of the psycho-social development of man from birth to death. In the words of Sudhir Kakar, "Erikson sees human development . . . as a series of predetermined steps or by which the individual seeks contact in an ever-widening radius with his society, which welcomes and regulates his unfolding."[8] Erikson's different conception of *ego* marks a departure from

Freud's 'originological' emphasis on childhood experiences in determining later behaviour. He sought to place *ego* in a historic-cultural context, that is, historical and cultural influences too act as determinants of one's *ego*. Fromm brings a historical perspective to the relation between the individual's psyche and society. He assigns a creative role to society in shaping human nature. He thinks that society has experienced a long series of 'historical dichotomies' by which he means the unconscious manifestation of ideology in society. The indefatigable nature of human mind always sought to resolve the incompatibilities occasioned by historical processes. The often passive acceptance of exploitative relationships between various classes of society, viewed in this light, fulfil an unconscious need. The self-preservative instinct compels man to grudgingly accept the conditions of his existence—the social norms, economic relations and other aspects. The introjection of societal standards makes him 'desire' what is absolutely 'necessary.' In other words the satisfaction of instinctual urges is culturally and socially determined. Fromm makes a powerful case for a synthesis between the biological and sociological forces. In their interaction man emerges as one who affects and is affected by history and social structure.

Thus in view of the obvious relevance of the above three psychoanalysts, Indian psychoanalytic critics do well to bring their theoretical formulations to bear upon their literary discussions. In fact a selective and systematized body of views of these three would serve as a theoretical frame of reference to the Indian creative writers and critics alike.

The next important aspect of psychoanalysis from which Indian fiction and criticism in English can benefit is its deep insight into the operation of myths in the mental sphere. India is a fertile land as regards both religious and literary myths. Myths have been often but uncritically employed by Indian novelists to strengthen the structure of the novels. Apart from Meenakshi Mukherjee, who has a chapter on the literary use of myths in her pioneering work *The Twice-Born Fiction,* no Indian critic of note has focused attention on this aspect of Indian fiction.

In psychoanalytic terms, the creative process involves a fusion of the writer's dreams with the material drawn from the psychological heritage of his race. No other elements of this heritage are more authentic and amenable to his genius than the myths of the race. Freud contended that myths are projected onto the supernatural phenomena after they have originated under purely human conditions. While the dreams of the writer are more in the nature of a personal fantasy myths constitute a universal illusion and by judiciously mixing elements from both, which a skilled writer is certainly capable of, proceeds aesthetic pleasure. The recognition of a widely shared human experience in the personal fantasy of the writer is the hall-mark of literary appreciation and a source of great pleasure. Peter Brooks thinks that every novelist works repetitions into his fictional product.[9] Myths are by nature repetitive and are applicable to a variety of people and circumstances. It can therefore be said that a psychoanalytic understanding of myths is doubly useful in the Indian context.

I would like to sum up my argument by stating that Indian fiction in English and Indian criticism in English are likely to be immensely benefited by incorporating psychoanalytic formulations into the creative and critical endeavour respectively. Psychoanalysis promises to introduce scientific spirit into the Indian literary critical effort which has been for long dominated by conventional and somewhat out-moded critical models. Psychoanalytic criticism is scientific to the core and is therefore in keeping with the scientific spirit of the present age.

NOTES

1. Meredith Anne Skura, *The Literary Use of the Psychoanalytic Process* (New Haven: Yale Univ. Press, 1981), p. 4.
2. Peter Brooks, "The Idea of a Psychoanalytic Literary Criticism," *Critical Inquiry,* XIII, 2 (Winter 1987), pp. 366-37.
3. Leonard Tennenhouse, ed., *The Practice of Psychoanalytic Criticism* (Detroit: Wayne State Univ. Press, 1976), p. 13.
4. Nayantara Sahgal in a letter to D. Ramkrishna, *Close Encounters with the Muse* (Eluru: Vecon Press, 1986), p. 86.
5. Sudhir Kakar, *The Inner World: A Psychoanalytic Study of Childhood and Society in India* (New Delhi: OUP, 1981), p. 6.
6. *Ibid.,* pp. 28-29.
7. Some of these traits have been painstakingly compiled by Indu Dave, *The Typical Indian Personality as Perceived by Indians* (Udaipur: Himanshu, 1984).
8. Sudhir Kakar, "The Traditional Hindu View and the Psychology of Erik H. Erikson," *Identity and Adulthood,* ed. Sudhir Kakar (New Delhi: Oxford Univ. Press, 1979), p. 3.
9. Peter Brooks, "Freud's Master Plot," *Literature and Psychoanalysis The Question of Reading: Otherwise,* ed. Shoshama Felman (Baltimore: The Johns Hopkins Univ. Press, 1982), pp. 280-300.

Spatial Vision in *Paradise Lost* and *Kambaramayanam*: A Comparative Perspective

K. CHELLAPPAN

Paradise Lost as myth enacts the archetypal story of separation and reintegration in terms of space, and the very form enacts this spatialization. Isabel McCaffrey has referred to the spatiality in the structure and texture of *Paradise Lost*. Our purpose is to relate the architectural design of *Paradise Lost* to its central vision of man, God and the cosmos and show how this design is manifested in the sequence and presentation of events as well as imagery, and how finally it aims at an aesthetics of poise absorbing dynamism. In this respect we shall compare *Paradise Lost* with *Kambaramayanam*, a Tamil epic written by Kamban somewhere between 11th and 12th century A.D. on the model of Valmiki's *Ramayana*, both dealing with the "Avatar" or descent of Rama into history for redemption of mankind and the triumph of God in the human form i.e. Rama over Ravana, who with all his greatness symbolizes demonic energy. The Tamil epic also attains a spatial vision by binding the kaleidoscopic flow of events in time and space into a simultaneity of perception symbolized by the still love and the dynamic poise of Rama, the basis and goal of all action in the epic. Rama is the still centre of the wheel still turning, both philosophically and structurally.

"Milton's imagination responds, as no other English poet's has responded with equal power, to the conception of infinite space." Though the Ptolemaic concept of the cosmos with stationary earth as the centre of heavenly bodies around which the Sun and Planets revolved must have appealed to his spatial imagination, he also spiritualized the spatial concept: he saw the infinity of space as suggestive of infinity or God himself.

Not only is Milton's God conceived in spatial terms, but the entire vision is made spatial, because everything is subordinated to the simultaneous perspective of God. To quote McCaffrey,

> Milton lives in the age of Descartes' spatial physics and Spinoza's geometric metaphysics; spatial imagining was part of his mental climate, . . . Writing of Heaven and the little heaven of paradise, Milton by a powerful releasing act of the imagination transposed the intuitive single glance of God into the poem's mythical structure. Our vision of history becomes, for the time being, that of the Creator "whose eye views all things at one view," (ll. 189-90) like him, we are stationed on a "prospect high Wherein past, present, future he beholds." (ll. 77-78) As Charles Singleton has written of the Divine Comedy: "This is a vision not of things as we should wish them to be but of things as they are. These are things which even before they are seen are submitted to the lap of God; and because of this, when they are seen they are objective. They do not stand in illusory space. They stand in the space that God stands in. The means of translating the story from time into 'God's space' are various."

The theme of *Paradise Lost*, i.e. harmony versus alienation, is brought out in relation to space. The very creation is a spatial extension of Heaven, and Hell, a parody of it. Harmony is Garden, and alienation, its loss. If God is pure consciousness, and the cosmos its fulfilment, Satan's alienated consciousness is conceived as hell. His is the archetypal journey of alienated consciousness. Whereas Adam and Eve before the fall are part of a cosmic harmony, Satan is always seen in antagonistic relationship to space. He is the explorer, conqueror, possessor because of the otherness within, and he cannot escape the categories of space he has himself invented, and whichever way he flies is Hell. It is this map-consciousness which he imports into the stillness of the garden, and his experience of Paradise is again seen as a spatial separation.

Satan's speeches show the infinity of hell experimented in the alienated consciousness. The dominant imagery is that of space and wandering. And his great soliloquy in *Paradise Lost*, Book IX, beginning with "O earth" (ll. 99-178) shows his obsession with place and the mind caught in the categories of space. And this soliloquy is preceded by the spatial journey itself. The journey down to the bottomless pit of his consciousness is always prefigured in spatial descriptions. Even his earlier reference to the mind as its own place separates mind from its external surroundings.

And this Satanic space is different from the infinity of God's space which is simultaneous, rhythmic and harmonious. The orchestration of the cosmos is reflected in the rhythmic dance of creation. If in a sense all action is spatialized in the Satanic perspective, there is another version of it in Heaven but now it is all seen simultaneously. That is, there are two kinds of spatialization: God's space seen as simultaneity and expansion and Satan's as succession, separation and alienation.

All creation is an extension of God's love and he is simultaneously and joyously present in all time and events he is the real though invisible force behind all his irony. This expansion is opposed to Satanic division and alienation. Whereas God found all creation good, Satan's incarnation as the serpent is a degradation and a contraction. God's identification with his creation is different from Satan's projection of his "agony" into others. His spatial separateness an eternity of pain, Satanic space thus becoming time. God's space absorbs or redeems time whereas Satanic space becomes the burden of time, and here as in other things we see the projection of the primal split—Satan's self division and his sense of separateness from God.

If in a sense all events are movements away or from a place, movement is an emanation of "that still point still moving." Infinity is seen as space, and the Satanic alienation is an experience of space experienced from outside and strangely but logically enough, time is also experienced as burden by him.

That is why we can say, that the Satanic event is symbolic of a split in space-time fusion. Possibly we could compare God's space absorbing time to the four dimensional space-time geometry of Minkovski whereas Satan's is spatialization in the objectionable sense: hence it is only time. His journeys are both horizontal and vertical, both in space and time, but the concept of time dominates over space, whereas in God's perspective, we find events being stripped of duration, and put together in a simultaneity of perception, and all events are horizontally linked, but suggesting the vertical axis of history. We may also say that all characters and events are horizontally linked with each other, and vertically with God.

Placed between the mighty opposites Heaven and Hell, is the poise of Eden, on the one hand a shadow of the splendours of God, and on the other facing the shadow of Satan, and here again there are differences in the vision of Eden in Books IV and IX. "This is the main configuration of the poem; from deep Hell upto the Mount of God, and down again to the subjected plains of alien earthly life." Corresponding to the background the action in both the crucial books shows the Edenic state as one of harmony and separation. Time is made still even in Book IV, but it does not have the pain of human time—of memory and desire as it is experienced by Satan. Their descent into the world of history is also a spatial movement and this spatial movement symbolizes man's separation from God. In both Book IV and Book IX God is very much present through absence, though in different ways. In Book IV the spatial concept—man as part of cosmos and Eden as part of the cosmic rhythm—is dominant whereas in Book IX, the time sense and the sense of object and possession-cum-movement are more dominant. Now the cosmos is seen through the chaotic self-consciousness of Satan. From now onwards movement to Adam and Eve means something different from the earlier rhythmic harmony, and Adam also chooses to have heaven in human terms. In Book IV, the imagery of inclusion and orchestration is dominant. Adam and Eve are part of each other, and both are willing parts of a larger whole, and this is symbolic of the total harmony. Phrases like *with thee* and *in thee* dominate and the discourse itself becomes concentric. Whereas in Book IV, Eden is seen as part of the cosmic harmony, just as every part of Eden is seen as part of a larger whole, in Book IX, there is an attempt by Satan to make the part the whole and he establishes a false analogy between Earth and God, and says, that

> Terrestrial heaven, danced round by other heavens
> That shine, yet bear their bright officious lamps,
> Light above light, for thee alone as seems
> In thee concentrating all their precious beams
> Of sacred influence as God in heaven
> Is centre, yet extend to all, so thou
> Centering recent from all those orbs. (ll. 103-9)

Satan's concept of the cosmos is geocentric, and the syntax betrays him as it tries to relate the centrality of Eden to that of God.

Similarly Adam and Eve tend to see themselves separate from each other, and both from Eden and ultimately from God. The part becomes the whole now, and the aesthetics of interpenetration and inclusion yields to the rhetoric of separation and alienation. When this sort of spatial consciousness comes to them, love becomes lust and Eve virtually becomes an object to Adam. To quote John Vernon, "Objects outside the body became objects of desire and consumption and the body too became an object. The Fall in particular is a fall into economic relationship since the body has first and foremost become an object of need and desire."

Corresponding to the spatial vision is the spatial structure of *Paradise Lost*. There is no sequential presentation of events—there is only presentation of places—Heaven and Hell in relation to each other, and Earth in relation to both. Against the mighty poise of Heaven we have the din of Hell, and in between the still serenity of Paradise. To quote McCaffrey, "The structure of *Paradise Lost*, if we look down upon all this world at once, is a great invented or, seen in three dimensions, a mountain with its roots in Hell and its crown in Heaven. We begin at the lowest point. We end at a point not quite so low, but far below the heights to which we have soared in the middle." Parallelism and juxtapositions are the major structural devices, and events are presented with an architectural weight. In a sense, the concept of Hegel and Whitehead that space is a relationship between events and objects is true here as far as the rendering is concerned.

The time-consciousness of the important characters as well as the presentation of events requires a spatial dimension though in different ways. In the words of Williams G. Madsen, "In the Garden before the Fall Adam exists, as it were, outside of history, exempt from the limitations of time. There is of course movement in Adam's universe, as Joseph Summer has shown, but it is Platonic cyclic movement, not Christian linear movement. It is the "Grateful vicissitude" of the "perpetual round" of light and darkness. (VI, 6-8) There is no change in Paradise, there is only "inter-change." (IX, 115) Even Raphael's speculation (in one of his few references to the future) about the destiny of unfallen man is Neoplatonic (V, 493-500) this is the familiar Neoplatonic doctrine of the vertical ascent through the scale of being, not the horizontal journey through "tract of time" that fallen mankind will have to make. This point is confirmed by Rosemary Syfret's excellent analysis:

> The focal point of the poem's place is the garden of Eden; of its time, the few days before, of, and after the fall. These focal points, the 'now' of its time, the 'here' of its place, radiate outwards through all time and all space; and all time and all space are continually focused inwards towards the 'here' and 'now' which they interfuse and play upon. The rapidly developing narrative of the events in hell and Satan's journey to earth drives the poem forward over indefinite stretches of human time to the central present of the few days in the garden of Eden. . . .
>
> All past and all future time have been contained and held within Adam's present and at the central point, determining the future and dividing it for ever from the past, is the moment of the fall in Book IX to which all the poem's past time has led and from which all its future flows. This concentrating and expanding rhythm is paralleled in the poem's spatial dimension. From the outermost bounds of the cosmos, hell at one extreme, heaven at the other, Satan and God look inwards to Adam and Eve at the centre in

Paradise.

This still point in the Garden of Eden is linked with the poise of Heaven, but in contrast to this the denizens of Hell are obsessed with time and the heavy change of their condition. But even their time consciousness is brought out through spatial imagery and in a crucial moment Milton says,

> That space the evil one abstracted stood
> From his own evil, and for the time remained
> stupidly good. (IX, 464-65)

Satan representing schizophrenia—a self-division which begins as a cosmic split, is now seen as separated from himself and the environment. Whereas God's time is spatial in the sense of simultaneity, Satan's is one of spatial oppression—an infinity of boredom and meaningless movement. Similarly events in Paradise partake of the harmony of Eden and the cosmos.

The object-consciousness and the time-consciousness along with self-consciousness come to Adam and Eve after the fall, and finally in relation to God and Christ they acquire a new perspective, and a new human togetherness which makes their descent into history, again portrayed as a spatial journey, meaningful if not rhythmic:

> Through the world's wilderness long wandered man
> Safe to the eternal paradise of rest. (XII, 313-14)

The long passage finds its culmination in 'the Paradise of rest.' The very sound effect shows that all movement leads only to the central poise and peace. Even thematically Adam only arrives at this wisdom or the dynamic poise of acceptance, "from now on I learn my lesson to obey." Equally important from this point of view is the conclusion:

> The world was all before them, where to choose
> Their place of rest, and providence their guide
> They had in hand loith wandering steps and slow
> Through Eden took their solitary way. (XII, 646-49)

The majestic movement of humanity into history is again towards the still point—and the human togetherness in relation to eternity imparts meaning to that movement itself. The passage reverberates with the sounds of steps in the corridors of history, but endowed with significance by the stillness of the Centre. The restoration of the significance of the wandering is paralleled by the restoration of the unity of the hands which were separated during the fall. The fall shows the separation of the land from the other parts of the body and Eve's hands from Adam's.

> Thus saying, from her husband's hand her hand
> Soft she withdrew, and like a wood-nymph light. (IX, 385-86)

Later too when she takes the forbidden fruit also the hand's separation is given prominence.

> So saying, her rash hand in evil hour
> Forth reaching to the fruit, she plucked, she ate: (IX, 780-81)

And in all this, *Paradise Lost* is very much like Kamban's *Ramayana*. Even though the entire story is enacted on earth, at the human level, it is only the shadow of the cosmic war between Gods and Demons. The agony of the Gods because of Ravana's egoism causes the descent of Vishnu as Rama from Heaven to Earth or Ayodhya (which is parallel to Christ's coming) and there is also the descent or the spatial journey of Rama from Ayodhya to Lanka through Panchavati. Lanka is the parody of Ayodhya, and Panchavati on the banks of the river Sarayu where Rama and Sita lead an Edenic life with Lakshmana before Ravana takes Sita, is the still point or the spatial centre of the epic. It is here the crisis of this epic takes place. This is caused first by Sita's intellectual error or curiosity on seeing the deer symbolizing falsehood and then by Rama's moral error in choosing to chase it, "obeying" the woman's desire. From our point of view, more important is Ravana's long and arduous journey from Lanka to Panchavati to abduct Sita which is comparable to the journey of Satan to Eden for a similar purpose. Parallel to this is Rama's journey to Lanka to "regain" Sita. It is God's quest for "the lost." Interestingly Sita is linked with earth and we can see a parallel between Ravana's "gathering" her in Panchavati which necessitates for the long journey seeking 'her through the world' (*PL,* IV, 271) with Eve's fall and the consequent journey. In this process Rama makes a visit to so many places. He redeems a number of people and restores the kingdom to Sugriva and Vibhishana who surrender at his feet. If Ravana's journey necessitates "history of time" Rama's feet redeem it and make it meaningful.

In one sense Rama moves towards all characters, but it is in response to the call of others. Therefore Rama is the unmoved mover behind all action, the real 'actor.' The central image of the epic is the feet of Rama moving across space and time, but it is equally true that it is only others who move towards his feet. Starting from Ahalya who is actually redeemed by the physical touch of Rama's feet, we find a number of characters, Guha, Sugriva and Vibhishana who seek the feet of Rama for their salvation but in that process, God also fulfils his purpose.

This is again comparable to the Christian view of human history as 'the working out not of Man's purpose but of God. God's purpose being a purpose for Man, a purpose to be embodied in human life, and through the activity of human life.' The Tamil epic deals with the philosophy of surrender as fulfilment of both Man's needs and God's purpose. There is a return and yearning of everything to the source and the epic as myth enacts this in its very form as Rama's cyclic return to Ayodhya and all his devotees' reunion with Rama. This is comparable to Milton's historical sense, which, "like St. Aug's combined a mythic awareness of the timeless City of God with a vision of the flux of centuries eddying round it in withdrawal and return. If history is the endless extension of the creative poise through which God fulfils his purpose, it is counterpointed by perennial movement of the creations back to the centre. Both the epics enact this dialectics of time and eternity, of man and God, though in different ways.

Rama's feet, 'still, but moving' symbolize poise and dynamism. It is interesting to note that the violent Bharata, his brother who is angry when his brother, Rama has to leave Ayodhya and is unwilling to become the king, finally agrees to keep the chappals of Rama, to symbolically reign over Ayodhya. And he waits for Rama for fourteen years, and it is the possibility of Rama's return that gives meaning to his waiting. Parallel to this is the waiting of Sita for Rama at Ashoka Vana in Lanka. Even though she could destroy Lanka, she chooses to wait for Rama. Rama's action is thus counterpointed by these waitings on the one hand, and the violent action of Ravana and other demons on the other. In a sense, even Ravana seems to be waiting for Rama's coming—all history waiting for the intervention of God. The philosophy of surrender and acceptance is there in all the characters and Rama also is conscious of the need to fulfil the pattern.

But there are significant differences between Kamban's view of time and history and Milton's. In Kamban, the characters are less conscious of time and history than in Milton. Separation does not make characters feel the tyranny of time; possibly because they are sure of the return of Rama. More than that: Kamban's view is more mythical than historical, and this is the fundamental distinction between the Hindu view of time which is more mythical and cyclical than the Judaeo-Christian view which is more historicist and linear. The memory of Satan can be compared with the agony and desire of Ravana; but there is more of mixing of memory and desire in the Satanic consciousness.

This leads us to the structural similarity between *Paradise Lost* and *Kambaramayanam.* Both can be seen as myths enacting a cyclical movement with emphasis on parallels and recurrences and 'time spirals rather than marches.' In both a core situation is repeated at various levels and there is a symmetry in the presentation of characters and events, in Heaven and Hell in one case, in Ayodhya and Lanka in the other. All the characters and events are horizontally linked with each other and vertically with God and Rama.

Just as at the thematic level the equilibrium of Rama's face is contrasted with the dynamics of all action around him, both of his devotees and enemies, aesthetically too, he is the embodiment of the *Santa Rasa,* the primal *rasa* underlying other emotions as embodied in the experience of other characters. Rama's is the experience underlying all experiences—he suffers nothing in suffering all and in this sense his serenity is comparable to the stillness of God and the sweetness of Christ in Milton. Rama's face is comparable to the red-lotus blooming in the picture because of equipoise. Aesthetically again, Kamban's *Ramayanam* too has an architectural weight and magnitude made of several elaborated scenes and similes. Even the presentation of the time-order of events has a similar pattern. In *Paradise Lost,* events have both simultaneity and succession. If Hell has a memory of the past, Heaven is endowed with foreknowledge in the early books, and Paradise becomes the eternal now. And again the fall is preceded by recapitulation which itself is a kind of vision, and the final vision also is only a reenactment of history. The future has already "happened." Even though in Kamban's *Ramayanam* memory does not play such an important role, events constantly look before and after, and action is also fulfilment of a pattern.

In Kamban's *Ramayanam* there is cosmic memory i.e. God as man vaguely remembering his heavenly status as well as the anticipation by the Rishis about the success of Rama which is comparable to God's prediction as well as Raphael's warning in *Paradise Lost.* If there is more time consciousness in Milton both in vision and in the ordering of events, there is also a greater redemption of time.

This sense of mass and movement, and mass as movement is there in the very texture of *Paradise Lost*. Not only is all movement described in imagery of space—caves, domes etc., but the very sound effect, the majestic movement of the verse and the semantic pattern created have this effect. We would like to mention in particular the effect of similes which link several characters in a simultaneity, but suggesting movement. For example, the simile comparing Eve to Oread, or Dryad of Delia's train and then to Pales or Pomera—shows the evolution of history but in a static way, and the characters seem to be waiting to plunge into history. The sense of movement is given an architectural weight both semantically and phonologically. The retarding effect is also meant only to add mass to movement and contributes to the dynamic poise of the epic. Kamban also uses both elaborate similes and a number of similes to illustrate one and the same point and his capacity for verbal elaboration and decorative is well known to the Tamil-speaking world.

The style and structure of *Paradise Lost* regain the space-time unity, the loss of which is the theme of the epic. God as pure act is pure space and time and in Satan we find the split of space and time experienced as motion and separation. And Adam and Eve participate in the stillness of God's space in the beginning and then move through 'movement' to the stillness of God's love.

In *Kambaramayanam* also the mythical form and its majestic style restore a primal unity of Rama and Sita and of Rama and his brothers and people at Ayodhya and the final vision of Rama's coronation with all his devotees is symbolic of this great synthesis. All surrender at the feet of Rama, while his serene face accepts and absorbs all.

To conclude, in *Paradise Lost*, its spatial vision and structure as well as the architectonic grandeur of its style suggest a kind of dynamic poise—energy absorbed by and pointing to stillness. And interestingly Kamban's *Ramayanam* also achieves a similar spatiality absorbing dynamism. And in one case we can see the prototype in the Dionysian dance acquiring Apollonian serenity and in the other the dance of Shiva, triumphing over and transmuting the primordial energy of Shakti into his equipoise and silence.

Satan and Ravana are uncontrolled energy in its endless movement and God and Rama are massive poise and there is a contrast between the joyous expansion of Good on the one hand, the expanded inversion of evil on the other. This is in tune with the philosophy of obedience as freedom in Milton and that of surrender as fulfilment in Kamban. But there are significant differences, as we have already indicated. Kamban's hero is both God and Man—or God as Man and there is less consciousness and redemption of time in the Indian epic than in Milton's Judaeo-Christian vision which accepts time because of its intersection with timelessness. Aesthetically also, Milton's poise is more dynamic, whereas Kamban's suggests a *shanti* and a serenity bordering on stillness.

A Realistic Look at Ramanujan's "A River"

K. SUMANA

Down the ages, poets all over the world have generally praised rivers for their beauty, majesty and grandeur. On top of that, they have glorified rivers and treated them with reverence. More so, Indian poets who have never been tired of eulogizing rivers and making obeisance to them.

But, A.K. Ramanujan, who unfortunately passed away at the age of 64, on July 14, 1994 in Chicago, U.S.A., made a radical departure from this age-old tradition of simply praising rivers. He does not give a traditional song of praise for the full river. In his famous poem, "The River," he makes a daring effort to penetrate beyond the veil of illusion and unfold the grim truth behind the devastation caused by the river in spate.

Before we come to the poem more in detail, we would do well to know a little more about A.K. Ramanujan, a poet we can justly be proud of.

Born in Mysore in 1929, Ramanujan was an eminent poet, linguist, translator, short story writer and a folklorist. He started his career as Lecturer in English at Mysore Maharaj College, Mysore. He sought to revolutionize Kannada grammar through his Ph.D. work. He moved to Chicago, U.S.A., in 1962. He was the Head of the South Asian Language Study in Chicago University, teaching four South Indian languages. He married Molly, a journalist and a writer, whose English novel he translated into Kannada entitled *Haladi Meenu.* He is survived by a son and a daughter.

Ramanujan is a distinguished Indian English poet of international repute. With his just two volumes of poetry—*The Striders* (1964) and *Relations* (1976)—he made a mark, achieving a synthesis of two cultures—ancient and modern, each illuminating and enriching the other. Ramanujan became a cult figure in Kannada literature with his anthology of Kannada poems—*Hokkulalli Hoovilla.* Each of his short stories in Kannada heralded a new era in Kannada literature.

Ramanujan was not only a distinguished poet, but also an eminent translator. Equally at ease with Tamil, Kannada and Telugu, he translated quite a few classics in these languages into English and vice versa.

To cite but a few instances, Ramanujan translated Alwar's 'Pasharams' from Tamil into English, U.R. Anantha Murthy's *Samskara* from Kannada into English and 'Kshetrayya pada' from Telugu into English. He also translated the Kannada mystic works of Akka Mahadevi and Basaveshwara into English under the title *Speaking of Siva.*

Now, coming back to Ramanujan's poem, "A River," it is about Vaikai which flows through Madurai, an ancient city of Tamil culture. He gives a graphic description of the river, ferociously flowing on the stones. He depicts

> the wet stones glistening like sleepy
> crocodiles, the dry ones
> shaven water-buffaloes lounging in the sun.

He shows no blind reverence to the river, but gives a realistic picture of it. The rise of water during flood may be exciting, but it also causes losses and damages to human life and property. The rising floods devoured

> One pregnant woman
> and a couple of cows
> named Gopi and Brinda, as usual.

We cannot enjoy flood when it kills human lives. The image of 'pregnant woman' is significant, for it involves two generations, the present and the future. So, the destruction caused by the river has deep and far-reaching consequences.

That is why, Ramanujan refuses to join the old poets who "sang only of the floods." Nor does he sail with the new poets who blindly follow the old poets in simply glorifying the river and flood. He sadly, but touchingly complains:

> no one spoke
> in verse
> of the pregnant woman
> drowned, with perhaps twins in her,
> kicking at blank walls
> even before birth.

The last passage of the poem sums up the earlier passages and the poet ironically says how

> the river has water enough

to be poetic
about only once a year.

What he means by this is that the river is beautiful when quiet in summer, but when it floods it causes untold suffering and misery that is not at all poetic.

The poet narrates the poem through the mouth of a visitor to make it objective. The greatness of the poem lies in the fact that the traditional praise for river has been contrasted with what is actually experienced by the people during the floods. Apart from presenting the grim realities of a river in spate, Ramanujan hints at the sterility of new Tamil poets who "still quoted the old poets." However, the images in the poem, particularly 'sleepy crocodiles,' 'shaven water-buffaloes,' 'pregnant woman' and 'identical twins' are full of significant suggestions for the future.

A Stylistic Approach to Ramanujan's "Still Another View of Grace"

C.L.L. JAYAPRADA

A.K. Ramanujan is an eminent poet and he is one of the best creative talents who have made their mark in Indian poetry in English. He delights in experimenting with language. His academic background in Linguistics gives him the necessary insight to handle language with alacrity and felicity without ever drifting into obscurity. Chirantan Kulshreshta has aptly commented that Ramanujan's poetry shows a 'chiselled workmanship.' According to R. Parthasarathy, his language is 'rapier sharp' and has a 'glass like quality.' He is one of the few Indian poets in English who could forge a distinctive and personal style and it is through his unique style he gives a sharp focus to his experience. A stylistic analysis of "Still Another View of Grace" by Ramanujan will illustrate how the poet achieves the meaning and particular aesthetic effects of the poem.

Stylistics uses the tools of linguistics for the analysis of works of literature. A stylistician accounts for the way a poem or a passage may strike the reader through his analysis unlike a linguist who is generally satisfied with the mere analysis of a piece of writing. For this reason, he speaks both in analytical and affective terms. Stylistics has tools to examine language at several levels—Syntax, Lexis, Phonology and Prosody. Poetry, in general, has close intra-textual relations and the language of a poem has a unified structure. Since Ramanujan's use of language in his poems is patterned at several layers, the study of the syntactic and lexical elements of the particular poem will be fruitful.

The poem and the analyses of its syntactic structure, nominal groups and verbal groups are given here. Some of the abbreviations used here are NP for noun phrase, VP for verb phrase, Prep for preposition, V for verb, Conj for conjunction, Adv for adverb, Neg for negative, Pron for pronoun, Quant for quantifier, Dem for demonstrative pronoun, Det for determiner, poss for possessive, Adj for adjective, Pres for present tense, Aux for auxiliary and so on. Since it is not possible to show the analysis of sentences in several layers as in a tree diagram, the symbol — is used for the higher level, the brackets and + are used for the lower level and)(brackets are used whenever brackets occur within brackets. Because sentences run fron one line to the other in poetry, * is indicated for run-on-constituents. And so NP* at the end of a line followed by another NP at the beginning of the next line indicates the continuation rather than the contiguity of two NPs. ij is a symbol for interjection and is used for the peripheral elements of language. Though prepositions are not immediate elements, they are shown in the syntactic analysis and are shown as part of Noun phrases only when they formed part of a tightly structured Noun phrase. Adverbs, prepositions and other marginal elements are not analysed in detail but when their use is significant, it is noted.

"Still Another View of Grace"

I burned and burned. But one day I turned
and caught that thought
by the screams of her hair and said: 'Beware.
Do not follow a gentleman's morals

with that absurd determined air.
Find a priest. Find any beast in the wind
for a husband. He will give you a houseful
of legitimate sons. It is too late for sin,

even for treason. And I have no reason to know your kind.
Bred Brahmin among singers of shivering hymns
I shudder to the bone at hungers that roam the street
beyond the constable's beat.' But there She stood

upon that dusty road on a nightlit april mind
and gave me a look. Commandments crumbled
in my father's past. Her tumbled hair suddenly known
as silk in my angry hand, I shook a little

and took her, behind the laws of my land.

Syntactic Structure of "Still Another View of Grace"

1 NP – VP (V) – Conj – VP (V). Conj – Adv – NP – VP (V +
2 Conj + V + NP +
3 Prep + NP + Prep + NP) – Conj — VP (V): VP (V)

4 VP (V + neg + NP +
5 Prep + NP).
6 VP (V + NP). VP (V + NP + Prep + NP +
7 Prep + NP). NP – VP (V + NP + NP *
8 Prep + NP). NP – VP (V + adv + adj + Prep + NP +
9 adv + Prep + NP). Conj – NP – VP (V + neg + NP – V) (infinitival) + NP).
10 (V)(infinitival)(+ NP + Prep + NP + NP + Prep + NP)
11 NP – VP (V + Prep + NP + Prep + NP (rel. cl = Pron + V + NP)
12 Prep + NP). Conj – NP – NP – VP (V +
13 Prep + NP + Prep + NP)
14 Conj – VP (V+NP+NP), NP – VP (V +
15 Prep + NP). NP – adv – V (infinitival)
16 Sub – NP (NP + Prep + NP), NP – VP (V + adv)
17 Conj – VP (V+NP+Prep + NP + Prep + NP).

Structure of Nominal Groups in "Still Another View of Grace"

S. No.	Line	Lexical Items	Structure
1	1	I	Pron (head)
2	1	one day	quant—N (head)
3	1	I	Pron (head)
4	2	that thought	dem—N (head)
5	3	the screams of her hair	det—N (Pre-modifier)-Prep. P. (Prep—Poss—N)(head)()
6	4	a gentleman's morals	det—Poss—N (head)
7	5	that absurd determined air	dem-adj-adj-N (head)
8	6	a priest	det-N (head)
9	6	any beast in the wind	det-N (head)—Prep. P (Post-modifier) (Prep-det-N)
10	7	a husband	det—N (head)
11	7	He	Pron (head)
12	7	You	Pron (head)
13	7&8	a houseful of legitimate sons	det-N (Pre-modifier)-Prep. P (head) (Prep+adj+N) (head)()
14	8	It	Pron (head)
15	8	sin	N (head)

16	9	treason	N (head)
17	9	I	Pron (head)
18	9	Your kind	Poss-N (head)
19	10	Brahmin	N (head)
20	10	singers of shivering hymns	N (head)—Prep. P (Post-modifier)(Prep+det+N)
21	11	I	Pron (head)
22	11	the bone	det—N (head)
23	11	hungers	N (head)
24	11 & 12	the street beyond the constable's beat	det—N (head)—Prep. P (Post-modifier) (Prep + det + Poss + N)
25	12	there	N (head)
26	12	she	Pron (head)
27	13	that dusty road	dem—adj—-N (head)
28	13	a nightlit april mind	det-adj-adj-N (head)
29	14	me	Pron (head)
30	14	a look	det—N (head)
31	14	Commandments	N (head)
32	15	my father's past	Poss—Poss—N (head)
33	15	Her tumbled hair	Poss—class—N (head)
34	16	silk	N (head)
35	16	angry hand	adj-N (head)
36	16	I	Pron (head)
37	17	her	Pron (head)
38	18	the laws of my land	det-N (head)-Prep. P. (Post-modifier) (Prep+Poss+N) (head)()

Structure of Verbal Groups in "Still Another View of Grace"

S. No.	Line	Lexical Items	Structure
1	1	burned	Past—V
2	1	burned	Past—V
3	1	turned	Past—V
4	2	caught	Past—V
5	3	said	Past—V

6	3	Beware	Pres—V
7	4	Do not follow	Pres—Aux—neg—V
8	6	Find	Pres—V
9	6	Find	Pres—V
10	7	will give	Pres—Aux—V
11	8	is	Past—V
12	9	have no (reason)	Pres-neg-V (+N)
13	9	to know	V (infinitival)
14	10	Bred	V (infinitival)
15	11	shudder	Pres—V
16	11	roam	Pres—V
17	12	stood	Past—V
18	13	gave	Past—V
19	14	crumbled	Past—V
20	15	known	V (infinitival)
21	16	shook	Past—V
22	17	took	Past—V

In the poem, Ramanujan presents an intimate experience and a personal crisis through the narrative mode. The poet or the persona encounters a prostitute in the street and despite his orthodox Brahmanical upbringing his defences fail and after a struggle he yields to the temptation. The poem has seventeen lines and four stanzas of four lines each and a single dangling line at the end, which has a clinching effect. The poem has a high proportion of nominal phrases, i.e., 39 nominal phrases and six embedded prepositional phrases. The proportion of the abstract nouns, 'that thought,' 'morals,' 'treason,' 'sin,' 'a nightlit april mind,' and 'commandments' is kept low despite the subjective nature of the experience presented. These formal features of the style contribute to the great visual quality of the poem.

Another significant feature of the poem is the way the denotative and connotative meanings merge and create new meanings without losing their original meanings. In the second sentence the object 'that thought' is an abstract noun but is referred to as 'her' in the next phrase. The words 'husbands' and 'sons' also give one the impression that the poet is talking about a lady. By subtle interaction of the abstract and concrete nouns, Ramanujan presents the common human predicament through the vivid delineation of a particular experience. The woman who appears here is a prostitute who roams beyond the constable's beat but she is also a thought, that thought which arises in one's mind, time and again, escaping the controls of conscious mind. 'Commandments' and 'walls,' suggested by the use of 'crumble' and 'behind' but they cannot contain the temptation once it is unleashed. One enchanting glance from her dissolves his determination in the flash of a second; his anger is quickly reduced to the shivering of uncontainable passion as her hair tumbles into his hand. The same mixing of the abstract and concrete nouns is evident in the neat balancing of 'shudder to the bone' and 'hungers that roam the street.'

There are altogether twenty-two verbs in seventeen lines—five verbs in the beginning of the poem and five in the end occur in the past tense. The rest of verbs which occur in the present tense indicate the change of mode from the narrative to the dramatic and all the sentences in which the present tense is used are in the imperative. The dramatic presentation lends authenticity and intensity to the experience presented. The finite verbs in simple structures contribute greatly to the succinct quality of the poem. The use of alliterative pattern in 'took' and 'shook' and 'wind,' 'kind,' 'land' and 'hand' and consonantal pattern with its repetition of constant sounds and clusters /Z/, /S/, /S/, /K/ and /St/, /zn/ give it a staccato rhythm reinforcing the emotion in the speaker's words.

The poet uses a number of short and pithy sentences in this poem and the last sentence left dangling at the end of the poem is foregrounded as if that is the 'Grace' given. The title "Still Another View of Grace" gives an ironic twist to the whole of the poem. Paradoxically it is not another view of sin but Grace and this indicates the poet's humanistic vision of life which accepts the absurd and irrational elements of life.

On the basis of the stylistic analysis of Ramanujan's poem, one can say with confidence that he is a remarkable and original craftsman. His predominantly nominal style, with the use of concrete nouns wherever possible, renders a visual quality and terseness to his poetry. He uses verbs with precision and economy, the structures of which vary greatly to suit the multiplicity of themes. The syntactic structures of his poems show remarkable variety and his stanza organization a complexity. On the basis of the study I assert Ramanujan richly deserves the praise he received from the critics for his craftsmanship and use of language. R. Parthasarathy is right in saying, "Ramanujan on the other hand has been able to forge an oblique, elliptical style all his own. . . . There is something clinical about Ramanujan's use of the language. It has a cold, glass-like quality. It is an attempt to turn language into an artifact." (*Ten Twentieth Century Indian Poets* [Delhi: Oxford University Press, 1976], p. 9.)

Anger Expression in Kamala Das's Poetry: A Study in *Klesa-Vritti*

G.D. BARCHE

Kamala Das's poetry has been examined and interpreted from different angles. For instance, Hari Mohan Prasad, disapproving of the other views of Das's poetry like 'a gimmick in sex' or 'striptease in words,' 'an over exposure of body' or 'snippets of trivia,' finally asserts: "But the truth is that her poetry is an autobiography, an articulate voice of her ethnic identity, her Dravidian culture."[1] M. Elias also holds a similar view: "Kamala Das is quite unique in exemplifying an allegiance to Dravidian India."[2] E.V. Ramakrishnan labels her as 'a confessional poet' and says "she has always dealt with private humiliations and sufferings which are the stock themes of confessional poetry."[3] Eunice De Souza forwards the same view: "Kamala Das writes incessantly about love or rather the failure of the love, her unhappy personal life, her unsuccessful sexual encounters and relationships."[4] On the other hand, A.N. Dwivedi is of the opinion that "she is aware of the world around her and gives a living expression of modern Indian woman's thoughts and feelings."[5] I.K. Sharma follows a different track and says: "Beneath the explosive poetry of Kamala Das . . . there flows a subterranean stream of bhakti heading towards its own destination to have an ideal lover, to attain higher truth like Mira."[6]

The different views above are given to show how scholars while interpreting Das's poetry catch hold of some isolated clue and jump to a certain conclusion. For instance, Das's poetry has a woman protagonist and the use of the personal pronoun 'I'. This makes E.V. Ramakrishnan and Eunice De Souza conclude that Kamala Das has presented love and sufferings of her personal life. Certain life incidents of the protagonist tally with those of Dravidian life pattern and this makes Hari Mohan Prasad and M. Elias see 'the ethnic identity.' The pain and suffering of the protagonist inspires I.K. Sharma to identify her with Mira. Any interpretation based on certain isolated feature makes its scope narrow and appeal shallow. Kamala Das's poetry is experientially deep and psychologically complex. Therefore, to understand her poetry in its true form, it becomes imperative to examine it through some more valid and objective approach.

A close reading of Kamala Das's poetry offers three things, viz., (i) its protagonist is a woman, (ii) she suffers immensely, (iii) this suffering surfaces specially through implicit or explicit anger expressions. And therefore, the basic question that arises is: why does she suffer? Kamala Das has made a sincere attempt to give an answer to this time-immemorial question through her protagonist. How has she done it? Consciously or unconsciously Kamala Das has successfully tried vedāntic philosophy, on the one hand, and Maharshi Patanjali's study of the human psyche, on the other. So before we take up Das's poetry for discussion in this new light, it is necessary to examine, in brief, the just-mentioned two aspects.

According to the vedāntic philosophy, the happiness is in the man or rather 'man' is happiness himself:

> raso vai sah rasam hi evāyam labdhwā ānandi bhavati
>
> (Taittiriya 2:7:1)

That is, man is happiness himself. He who returns to this true abode of his, shall always be happy. This view is further affirmed in Brihadāranyaka upanishad:

> Etasyaiva ānandasya sarve jivah mātram upjivanti. (4:3:32)

It means, it is this ānand that is at the base of all life. However, unfortunately man gets deprived of this ānand and he suffers. So the next allied question is: why does he lose this birth bound gift of ānand? Brihadāranyaka has answered this question as follows:

> yasca srotriyo' vrijino' kamahato' thaisa eva parama ānandāh.

That is, all the bliss is for one who is full with vedic wisdom, detachment and desirelessness. In other words, man suffers, if he does not have real knowledge, detachment and desirelessness.

Maharshi Patanjali has reiterated this view of suffering of man. Of course he has put it slightly differently. According to him man gets deprived of joy or ānand owing to his unbridled citta vrittis. He talks of five vrittis of mind which may fully or partially cause klesa (suffering): "Vrittayah pancatayyah klistāklistāh." (P.Y.I: 5) This sutra (compact expression) states three facts: (i) the vrittis are five in number, (ii) they may be highly or slightly less klesakārak (misery causing), (iii) the word

'Klista' would mean painful or misery caused owing to the vrittis' association with one or more klesas or when the vrittis get closely associated with klesas, they become 'klista,' i.e., they cannot be done away with or removed. Further he names Vrittis as "Pramānaviparyaya vikalpa nidrāsmritayah." (P.Y.1:6) That is, pramāna (right knowledge), viparyaya (wrong knowledge), vikalpa (imagination), nidra (to think of what has not yet happened or been experienced), smrtayah (plural of 'Smrti' which means to think of what has already happened or been experienced). Patanjali also talks of five klesas: "Avidyā smitārāgad vesābhinivesāh klesah." (P.Y.2:3) That is, avidyā (erroneous knowledge), asmitā (I-amness or I-consciousness), rāga (attachment), dvesa (hatred), abhinivesa (intentness) are klesas. The term 'klesa' has to be understood both as an agent as well as consequence.

The above mentioned facts can be summed up thus: to operate in some direction or in some way is the basic nature of human mind. However, when certain vritti (tendency) or vrittis recur and finally get entrenched, they become predominant and get associated with one or more klesas (deep disturbing feelings). The ultimate result is klesa (pain and suffering). Thus according to the upanishads, it is the absence of real knowledge: (srotriyo), and according to Patanjali the presence of false knowledge (viparyaya) which culminate in klesas like 'asmitā' (I-consciousness) and dvesa (the feeling of sorrow) and which collectively cause human suffering.

With this brief discussion of the concept of ānand, the causes of its deprivation and the final consequence, let us turn to Kamala Das's poetry. It has been said earlier that the protagonist in her poetry is a woman and she suffers vastly. The discussion above makes the cause of her suffering traceable. It is seen above that the pleasure (ānand) is in the person himself. But then the protagonist here tries to see it outside in man. She develops this view because she is governed by the viparyaya vritti. This vritti is defined by the great rishi as "Viparyaya mithyājnanamata-druppapratistham." (P.Y.1:8) That is, viparyaya is false understanding or knowledge. In viparyaya the real nature of the object or phenomenon is not realized because of the false knowledge or notion owing to some bias. For instance, Gloucester in *King Lear* takes Edgar for a villain, becomes angry and unnecessarily suffers.

In the present case the protagonist of Das's poetry is in search of happiness. She doesn't know that happiness is inside her only. On the contrary, she looks upon man as a source of pleasure surely owing to the viparyaya vritti. But when she actually transacts with man, she doesn't get the preconceived pleasure. Naturally now the problem is that the picture of man that she had conceived, and the picture of man that emerges after her contact with him don't fit in. The more she tries to see the man of her imagination in the actual man she encounters, more miserable she becomes. This situation makes her suffer from the klesa, viz., dvesa, Maharshi Patanjali has defined dvesa as: 'dukhānusayi dvesah.' (P.Y.2:8) That is, the feeling resulting from suffering in dvesa. Here the protagonist's failure to have happiness (ānand) from the man fills her with dvesa, i.e., the feelings of hatred and anger. And one repeatedly notices these explosive feelings being expressed through the anger expressions in Das's poetry.

A close reading of Kamala Das's poetry reveals the fact that most of her poems are full of the feelings of anger and scorn. In some poems anger oozes, as it were, from every word and every line. Let us begin with a few lines from her well known poem "The Old Playhouse":

> you were pleased
> With my body's response, its weather, its usual shallow
> convulsions. You dribbled spittle into my mouth, you poured
> yourself into every nook and cranny, you embalmed
> My poor lust with your bitter sweet juices.[7]

The deep-seated anger and hatred get here very effectively expressed through the assertive structures and further highlighted by the pauses. Besides, it is the best example of viparyaya vritti of human mind. And to understand this fact, the explanation follows: A really great creative artist gives only half the fact leaving the other half for the reader's imaginative faculty. Above, the poet has given only one side, that is, the beloved's reaction, and the other half has to be restructured by the reader. One may ask the questions like: Was the lover really pleased with the beloved's body response? Was he dribbling spittle into her mouth? And so on. The answers may further vary according to the reader's experiences. But the fact is that the lover must have gone through the usual process of love making. However, the protagonist sees something obnoxious in his actions. This situation can properly be understood thus: a cracker bursts the moment it is lit with fire. But one also knows that it bursts not because of the fire alone but the powder inside it. Similarly, the anger and hatred manifested by the beloved is not solely planted by the lover. It is very much present in her, though in the dormant or suppressed form. It simply surfaces when she transacts with her lover. And she, owing to her viparyaya vritti, sees the cause of suffering in him. This is a proved psychological fact that pleasure or suffering is due to the in-present sanskāras of the mind. Coleridge has also put it in a very simple form in his poem: "Dejection: An Ode":

I may not hope from outward forms to win
The passion and the life, whose fountains are within

In "Composition" we see another aspect of viparyaya vritti of mind. After getting married, the protagonist got full freedom from her husband. Initially she hesitated, but started enjoying the freedom liberally until she grew suspicious about her husband's intention behind granting her full freedom. And so she asked him:

I asked my husband,
am I hetero
am I lesbian
or am I just plain frigid?
He only laughed.

Here the anger expression is evident through the interrogative structures coupled with the ironical tone. The fact is that the moment the husband gave her full freedom to enjoy, he, too, got the same to enjoy. But when she notices this, she thinks that somewhere she is responsible for his grazing green pastures outside. She imagines that he wanders away because she might be a hetero, a lesbian or a frigid. Actually the husband's pleasure trips outside are by right and this is obvious from his reaction: 'He only laughed.' But then she unnecessarily constructs mental pictures of flaws in her and thereby gets upset and annoyed.

In "The Freaks" first she gives a very ugly picture of her lover and then wonders why he can't give the real joy to her. Let us examine the following lines.

He talks, turning a sun-stained
Cheek to me, his mouth, a dark
Cavern, where stalactites of
Uneven teeth gleam, . . .
. . . can this man
With nimble finger tips unleash
Nothing more alive than the
Skin's lazy hungers?

The basic question is: where is joy? Where is beauty? The vedantic answer is "Yathā atra tathā anyatra," i.e., what is inside, the same is outside. Othello was a tall black moor, but Desdemona could see unparalleled beauty in him. She fell in his love and eloped with him. And here the protagonist sees her lover's colour as 'sun-stained' and his mouth as 'dark cavern'; and his love-making gives her only the skin-deep pleasure. The natural consequence is 'dvesa' (the feeling of anger and anguish). The trouble with this woman is that due to her viparyaya vritti she sees beauty in the man's outward physical appearance and joy in the physical process of love-making. That is, she tries to see that which is not there.

The operation of viparyaya vritti in yet another direction can be seen in "Gino." Look at the following lines:

> This body that I wear without joy, this body
> Burdened with lenience, slender toy, owned
> By man of substance, shall perhaps wither battling with
> My darling's impersonal lust.

The pain and anger is evident in the repetition of the phrase 'this body' and the use of the phrases like 'burdened with lenience,' 'men of substance,' 'battling with.' The cause is obviously the false picture-making tendency of the protagonist's mind. The fact is that one does not wear one's body. It is the very dharma, the nature of the body to wear away with or without joy with the passage of time. Secondly, it is not the body, but the soul of its joy. However, here the lady fully identifies herself with the body and its operations. Then, she holds the impersonal lust of her lover responsible for her suffering. But the fact is that it is the universal spirit within and without that governs all the operations. And her failure to see this fact makes her suffer. This point is further elaborated in the following paragraph.

Kenopanisad begins raising the basic question: "Kenesitam patati presitam manah" i.e., who impels man to do something? And then the answer given is "Brahma" or "The supreme power." But then man generally identities himself with what he does. And this gives birth to another klesa—"Asmitā." Mahamuni Patanjali has defined it as 'drgdarsanasaktayor ekatmatevāsmitā.' (P.Y.2:6) That is, when one superimposes one's own physical self upon the supreme self, it produces asmitā (ahama bhava) or Ego or I-consciousness. And it is this Ego that causes klesa (suffering). In the foregoing instance, the cause of suffering is obviously this 'I-consciousness.' This can further be seen in the following lines from "An Introduction":

> It is I who laugh, it is I who make love
> And then feel shame, it is I who lie dying
> With a rattle in my throat. I am sinner,
> I am saint. I am the beloved and the
> Betrayed.

Here is the best intergrafting of the protagonist's fallacy and failure fomenting her frustration. 'I-consciousness' on the one hand, and the failure, on the other, generate bitterness in her. And this feeling is very powerfully expressed through the repetition of the personal pronoun 'I' and the use of the parallel but contrary words like: make love—feel shame, sinner—saint, beloved—betrayed. This suffering obviously springs from her wrong knowledge about the 'self.'

How viparyaya vritti can turn 'heaven' into 'hell' can be seen in the following lines from "Convicts":

> We lay
> On bed, glassy eyed, fatigued, just
> The toys dead children leave behind,
> And we asked each other, what is
> The use, what is the bloody use?
> That was the only kind of love,
> This hacking each other's parts
> Like convicts hacking, breaking clods
> At noon.

Here the life-refreshing process of 'love making' and its blissful conclusion are depicted in the most horrible form. The protagonist sees convicts's actions of 'hacking, breaking clods' in the love-making process; and 'fatigue' and 'death' in the post love-making phase. Here the two tier problem of this woman is evident, viz., first, she does not have the pleasure (ānand) within, second, her mind, being governed by viparyaya vritti, builds negative pictures. The natural outcome is bitterness that drips from the frightful images like glassy eyed, fatigued, the toys dead children leave behind, convicts hacking, breaking clods, etc.

The power of viparyaya vritti of human mind generating klesa like 'asmitā' (I-consciousness) and dvesa (suffering) and finally ending in anger and pain can best be seen in the following lines from "The Stone Age":

> . . . ask me the flavour of his
> mouth, ask me why his hand sways like a hooded snake
> before it clasps my pubis. Ask me why like
> A great tree, felled, he slumps against my breast,
> And sleeps. Ask me why life is short and love is
> Shorter still. Ask me what is bliss and what is its price.

The recurrence of the imperative structures with accusative pronoun 'me' halted by the speed breakers, viz., and full periods very vividly ventilate the subterranean suffering of the protagonist. The two-fold nature of the cause of her agony is here evident. First, the pictures of love, lover and her own self that she had conceived and the reality she encounters and experiences instead of matching collide. Second, she falsely thinks that she is capable to answer all sorts of questions; the reality is that she isn't and she can't. And this constitutes the crux of her problem. Had she really had the real knowledge of love and life and had she been really competent to answer all the questions, there would have been no cause for her suffering and the resultant pain and anger.

The whole discussion can be summed up thus: the feeling of anger forms the nucleus of Kamala Das's poetry. This anger stems from pain and suffering. The suffering is caused by klesas, viz., dvesa and asmitā. And these klesas are produced and nourished by viparyaya vritti, on the one hand, and the absence of the real enlightenment through the study of the classics like Upanishads, the *Bhagavad Gita,* the dramas of Shakespeare, etc. Such is the complex nature of the ruling passion of anger in Das's poetry. It is fed individually by the factors like the viparyaya vritti, the klesas, the absence of the real enlightenment through the classics, etc., as well as collectively by all of them together.

NOTES

1. Hari Mohan Prasad, ed., *Indian Poetry in English* (New Delhi: Sterling, 1985), p. 3.
2. M. Elias, "Kamala Das' and Nayar Heritage," *JIWE,* Vol. 6 (July 1978), p. 23.
3. E.V. Ramakrishnan, "Kamala Das as a Confessional Poet," *JIWE,* Vol. 5 (Jan. 1977), p. 29.
4. Eunice De Souza, "Kamala Das" in *Indian Poetry in English: A Critical Assessment,* ed. Vasant Shahane and M. Sivaramakrishnan, (Delhi: Macmillan, 1980), p. 41.
5. A.N. Dwivedi, *Indian Poetry in English; A Literary History and an Anthology* (New Delhi: Arnold Heinemann, 1983), p. 122.
6. I.K. Sharma, "Mary and Mira: A Study of Kamala Das" in *Studies in Indian Poetry in English,* ed. O.P. Bhatnagar (Amravati, 1981), pp. 74-75.
7. Kamala Das, *The Old Playhouse and Other Poems* (New Delhi: Orient Longman, 1973).

The Romantic Redeemer and the Blighted World: A Re-reading of Shelley's *Prometheus Unbound* and Tagore's *Red Oleanders*

NILA DAS

From the earliest phase, mythology, religion and literature all over the world have recorded the human craving and prayer for deliverence, both individual and collective, from the paradoxical, death-haunted existential situation, and the forms of evil, moral and natural. Commonly there has been a belief in a *soter* or saviour, divine or human, a model of perfection, who would preserve the cosmic order, make human life harmonious, and the society a renewed blessed state. Etymologically, the word salvation suggests "making whole."[1]

In the post-Renaissance culture of doubts and rationalistic prophecies, the Redeemer myth and the religious and cultural ultimates it stood for, increasingly became incidental, a nostalgia or dream rather than a prerogative or 'complete vision.' The myth is revived or recreated by the Romantics. Sharply reacting to the "imperialism" of matter and machine, weary in a world where "youth grows pale and spectre thin and dies/Where but to think is to be full of sorrow . . . /Where beauty cannot keep her lustrous eyes," the Romantics once again and all the more intensely, crave for the blessed state, when existence would become "a symphony and song," a realm of beauty and beatitude.

Inclined as they are, to "leave the world unseen" on "the viewless wings of poesy," if and when the Romantics meet the mundane reality, they often do in terms of their vision of the reality beyond. The Redeemer myth, the Superman in Romantic terminology, provides (not always) the stop-gap.

The present paper focuses on two plays, Shelley's *Prometheus Unbound* (1820)[2] and Tagore's *Red Oleanders* (1925).[3] In both the plays the poet-dramatists use the Redeemer myth, carved out of their Romantic agony and passion for a new earth and life. The interest in this paper is in whether and how far the poets of the West and the East join hands to encounter and overcome the socio-existential inauthentic.

II

Shelley believes that there is an omnipotent benevolent power "which visits with its breath our silent chord at will," "which connects not only man with man, but with everything which exists." Shelley calls the power God, the Spirit of Nature, the Spirit of Love.[4] The perfect life in Shelley's conception would be or could be attained, when man realizes this 'power' within him; and his "loftier instincts," the "kindly passions" with "changeless nature coalescing," undertake regeneration's work. The incentive would come from the "higher man," imbued with "pure desire," "universal love," "the elevated will."[5] Christ is a model. Prometheus another.

A self-proclaimed Shelleyan in his early days, and a transcendentalist idealist by training, Tagore too has his faith pinned on a Supreme Being:

> In man we see revealed *Bhuma,* the Supreme Being. . . . He is travelling the royal road of eternity, undeterred by disease or distress, danger or death. Universal Nature has put her garland around his neck. The light of knowledge is shining on his high forehead.[6]

Those who have the *Bhuma* "enthroned" in their "hearts,"

> In the narrow path of New Life
> They are the forerunners, ignoring all limits
> Conquering the impossible.
> In every step resound the great "Yea."[7]

Red Oleanders pictures such forerunners in a blighted world.

III

In *Prometheus Unbound,* the setting is mythical and also modern, perhaps post-modern or futurist as well. The Earth is eroded, "Black, wintry, dead, unmeasured; without herb/Insect or beast, or shape or sound of life/ . . . No change, no pause, no hope." (21-24) The environment suffers the blight as much as do the human beings. Men are slaves, requited for "knee-worship, prayer and praise/And toil, and hecatombs of broken hearts." (7-8) In *Red Oleanders,* a play written a century later, the wasteland is presented in a similar key, if only in more recent terms. Materialism and greed, dictatorial power and iron mechanism have turned Yaksha Town, a city of goldmines, into a death-trap. Nature is no longer nourished, nor does she nourish humankind. Men and women are treated as faceless numbers. The *Town* culture flourishes on exploitation, fear, destruction, death. The Yaksha Town is the contemporary collapse of civilization in nucleus.

In Shelley's play, the dead-alive Earth and the elements look forward to Prometheus, not the legendary heaven-defier, proud and revengeful, but the Shelleyan angel, the "spirit of keen joy" (as the Earth says), "the highest perfection of moral and intellectual nature impelled by purest and the truest motives" (as the dramatist notes)[8] as their Redeemer. Contrary to their expectations, however, the play shows Prometheus himself as a *salvato salvandus,* a saviour in need of salvation. Even after three thousand years of effort to master patience and endurance, his chosen weapons against the powers of Darkness and Disharmony, he is yet visibly effected by the hounding Furies, both inner and outer. He flares up in revenge ("these pale feet . . . might trample thee/If they disdained not such a prostrate slave," I.49-52) gives way to vaingloriousness ("Mother . . . thou/Scorn him, without whose all-enduring will . . . / thou had vanished" I.113-17). In the context, self-control is a mark of superior person or conversion. It is evident that in the art of self-mastery Prometheus still has a long way to go.

In *Red Oleanders* too, the dead-alive populace crave for a new mode of life, free and fearless, joyous and vivacious, unbarred from the "green of the woods," the "gold of sunshine," "the open sky." Ranjan incarnates their dream, and their sense of freedom. He is *joie de vivre,* knows the magic of lifting the pressure of mechanistic labour, of making the dead country singing in glee. It is said that the source of Ranjan's power lies in the laws of Nature.[9] In this, he counterpoints the tyrant king of the metallic world, who has subjugated Nature, and, in the course, has himself turned anti-Nature, having made Nature caught in a self-destructive network, her magic of creation lost.

Unlike in *Prometheus Unbound*, the bewailing lot in *Red Oleanders* hardly turn to Ranjan, the person, for their release. In fact, Ranjan hardly enters the stage. But his powerful presence is felt in the air and in the mind of everybody, both the torturers and the tortured, and especially in every step and word, thought and dream of Nandini, his lady-love and activating force. According to some Tagore critics, Ranjan is not an actual human being, but an idea, or an impulse.[10]

Prometheus moves towards self-emancipation in the typical Romantic way. He detaches his mind from the agonizing immediate and remembers the happy life he once had in company of Asia, when the earth was beautiful. In one interpretation, if Prometheus represents human mind, intellect, understanding, Asia embodies eternal love. Knowledge alone does not bring regeneration, without the help of love.[11] The very thought of love, beauty, joy restores peace to Prometheus' disturbed soul. Rage and hatred evaporate. His emotions purified, he repents of his curse, forgives himself for what he has been, a defiant, self-conscious being: "Grief for a while is blind, and so was mine/I wish no living thing to suffer pain." (I.303-5) It is a miraculous metamorphosis. The intervening stages of the spiritual progress missing, how far it is convincing is an open question.

Unlike the Shelleyan Redeemer, Nandini, Ranjan's alter-ego, Shelley's Asia with a difference, needs no redemption by herself. She is less of a flesh and blood individual, say some critics. An incarnation of joy and love (the very name means one who brings joy), she vitalizes the machine-ridden Yaksha Town with the "joy of Nature," the "rhythm of life." Her very presence initiates a miraculous transformation among the people. The Professor, buried in his mechanical calculations, finds himself dreaming of a different kind of life: "She has for her mantle, the green joy of the earth. That is our Nandini. . . . Midst the clamour of the market place, she is the tuned up lyre. My attention flies away . . . like a bird." (202) To Bishu, the mystic ministrel, Nandini brings the nostalgia for the life beyond: "The pain of desire for the near belongs to the animal, the sorrow of aspiration for the far belongs to man. That faraway flame of my eternal sorrow is revealed through Nandini." (63) To others, wearing red oleanders in her hair, her "weapon of love," Nandini looks like an "ominous" spark of revolt. In contrast to Shelley's self-conscious elite hero, Nandini is hardly conscious of what she is. She is rather what others have thought or imagined her to be. The desire for a perfect life and earth resides in every heart. Nandini is that desire. She is the seed of redemption, aesthetic rather than ontological, planted in every soul. Is aesthetic redemption all or enough to transform a social mechanism? The question is not answered.

Himself redeemed, Shelley's Redeemer does not know the world. The ungenerate Earth notices Prometheus' change, alarmed: "No, thou canst not hear/Thou art immortal, and this tongue is known/only to those who die." (I.149-57) Prometheus is unperturbed. He seems to have attained a supra-consciousness or self-sufficiency, when the glamours of the world do not reach him any more. Even while Mercury and the Furies unleash a horrible train of tortures, Prometheus dreams of a renewed universe, blossoming in truth, peace, love, liberty. Prometheus' encounter with the Furies is really a dialogue across two incommunicable realms.

Nandini challenges the King of Machines in sharper, if equally

Romantic, terms.[12] But the clash between the two fades out as the Tagorean tyrant, a Romantic visionary at heart, and weary of the overgrown power he himself wields, waits for the hour, when the Nandini impulse will bring him salvation: "On the day when you can arrive full sail . . . the hour of welcome will strike. Even if the wind be a storm, all will be well." (31)

In Shelley's play, the dethronement of evil and the draw of "perfect life" are simultaneous. While the "almighty tyrant" succumbs to Demogorgon, the Eternal Necessity without the least resistance, Prometheus, formally released by Hercules, is reunited with Asia, Panthea, Ione, the Earth, the Spirits. The Spirit of Life merging with the Spirit of Love, the world changes instantaneously: "thrones were kingless/ . . . None frowned, none trampled; hate, disdain or fear/Self-love or self-contempt, on human brows/No more inscribed." (III.IV.130-35) It is the Millennium established in a miracle. The Spirits rejoice over the dawn of the new era. The Chorus join them. Demogorgon greets new life:

> Gentleness, Virtue, Wisdom and Endurance
> These are the scale of that most firm assurance
> Which bars the pit over Destruction's strength. . . .
> Good, great and joyous, beautiful and free;
> This is alone Life, Joy, Empire, and Victory

More of a wish or an idea than a reality, Demogorgon's crescendo unwittingly indicates the failure of the Earth to earn the changed condition. It is an old truism that virtue and knowledge are attained by persistent approximation. Throughout *Prometheus Unbound,* the Earth and mankind, impatient and bewailing as they have been, have hardly striven for the wisdom or the elevation, when they "will that there would be no evil and there is none."

Red Oleanders ends on an almost opposite strain. The King decides to open his everclosed doors to Nandini. His own officers, the Furies of the machine world, resenting the King's transformation, make him kill Ranjan unawares. Nandini sees Ranjan lifeless and screams out, for once, in her womanly earthly voice: "King, they all say you know magic. Make him wake for my sake." (164) The King's reactions vary from shock, anger to lamentation, repentance: "My machine can put an end to waking. —Alas: I know not how to awaken." (164) Nandini launches her war in full scale against the machine world. In a sudden, but not too unexpected move, the King himself offers to be her companion. Nandini's passionate, pathetic voice rings like a prayer for the victory of

Ranjan: "He leaves behind him in death his conquering call. He will live again. . . . I did await his coming, and he did come. I still wait to prepare for his coming again, and he shall come again." (173) The masses of the Yaksha Town join her, although doubts remain if they share her faith. In fact, a sceptical voice is heard in the melee: "Shall we be able to win through?" (175) to which the more experienced King has a ready answer: "we shall at least be able to die! . . . I have found the meaning of death. I am saved." (175) Penance is a way to salvation. To equate personal salvation with social redress is a Promethean task that neither the King nor Nandini has the potentiality to perform.

IV

For the solitary poets, and specially Romantic poets, to provide a key to both salvation and social change has never been easy. Neither Shelley nor Tagore has succeeded in transmitting his ideas about the regeneration of life and the world in convincing dramatic terms. They have not been able to create a new myth or prototype of the Redeemer either. Ranjan and Nandini remain mostly a dream, a nostalgia and a desire. Prometheus is himself redeemed by a miracle and has the world transformed by another miracle. Yet, the very fact that both the poet-dramatists emphasize the need for an inner change, from self-centred, self-defeating negativity and defiance to all-embracing love and compassion, as a pre-condition of a harmonious life, both social and spiritual, is a legacy not to be minimized. That man is perfectible, that he can redeem himself by being united with his own "higher nature" and with the Nature at large, is a faith one cannot afford to abandon either.

Both Shelley and Tagore speak of an ideal civilization rather than an actual alternative society. Perhaps in our world of tottering alternatives, the received structure of experience is no longer valid. Perhaps the truth of life lies in man's dissatisfaction with here and now, and his craving for the not-yet. Perhaps it can survive the destruction of the belief that man is bound some day to live like a god in a perfect world.

NOTES

1. "Soteriology," *The Encyclopedia of Religion,* ed. Mircea Eliade (New York: Macmillan, 1987).
2. *Shelley: Poetical Works*, ed. Thomas Hutchinson (Oxford, 1970).
3. Rabindranath Tagore, *Red Oleanders: A Drama in One Act*

(Macmillan, 1926).

4. "Essay on Christianity," "On Love," *Shelley's Literary and Philosophical Criticism,* ed. John Shawcross (London: Humphry Milford, 1932). "Notes on Hellas," "Queen Mab."
5. "Queen Mab," "A Philosophical View of Reform," *Shelley's Prose,* ed. David Lee Clark (London: Fourth Estate, 1988).
6. "The Master's Will be Done," *Towards Universal Man* (Asia, 1962), p. 200.
7. "The Forerunner," *Later Poems of Rabindranath Tagore,* trans. Aurobindo Bose (London: Peter Owen, 1974).
8. Shelley, Preface to *Prometheus Unbound.*
9. Not a mechanistic process, in Tagore's philosophy, Nature is an "emergent creation," an evolved "value" in the mass of material. The Infinite Self manifests/realizes Himself through both His creations, Nature and Man, each a unity, and yet intimately related to each other. In order to reach perfection, to realize the Infinite within oneself, one needs to accept and tune oneself with Nature. To treat Nature as a means is subtle form of negation, and negation defeats the aim of salvation. Tagore, *The Religion of Man* (London: Unwin, 1975).
10. Abu Sayeed Ayyub, "Is That Your Delight?" *Visva-Bharati Quarterly*, 41.1-4 (May 1975-April 1976).
11. Frederick A. Pottle, "The Role of Asia in the Dramatic Action of *Prometheus Unbound,*" *Shelley: A Collection of Critical Essays,* ed. George M. Ridenour (Prentice Hall of India, 1980).
12. "Don't you hear . . . the autumn song . . . Come out King! Out into the fields." (20) "The living heart of the earth gives itself up in love and life and beauty. When you rend its bosom . . . you bring up with your booty the curse of its dark demon. . . . The curse of grabbing and killing." (21)

Disillusionment and Social Change: A Re-reading of Badal Sircar's *Evam Indrajit*

MOUTUSHI CHAKRAVARTEE

Parameters of social change are variously determined depending on the historical, political and psychological forces. What was happening in the Indian socio-cultural ethos in the 1960s finds reflection in the theatre of the period, for the dramatic art is communal.[1] The euphoria of Independence was over. Growing up in the new set-up meant admitting facts that were contrary to one's beliefs. Hopes were belied, expectations frustrated: idealism came in direct confrontation with realism. People were, by and large, disillusioned. With this disillusionment and a new social awareness, a dramatist appeared to be better equipped than ever before to "cast a cold eye on life"[2] and thus tackle problems with discussion and debate.

Playwrights like Sharad Joshi, Girish Karnad, Mohan Rakesh, Badal Sircar found conflict—that important ingredient of drama (as enunciated by Shaw, "no conflict, no drama"[3])—between the life that is lived and the one that ought to be lived. Social values were crumbling, and thinking people found themselves lost. There was conflict between traditional ways and the new middle-class attitudes. Reconciliation appeared a far cry although efforts persisted.

Out of this unenviable situation emerges *Evam Indrajit*.[4] The play portrays how difficult adjustments are when hopes of yesterday clash with those of today. At the rise of the curtain, we encounter two persons: Auntie and the Writer. Quite unconventionally, the Writer faces not the auditorium but the wall, his back to the audience. Auntie's concern, understandably, is the food which the Writer did not have since the morning as he was 'scribbling.' His conversation with Manasi, a little later, focusses different interests of the two women separated by a generation. The latter wants to know of the progress of the writing, least concerned about the food. Sircar, like all new playwrights (e.g., Ibsen, Shaw, Brecht), is discarding conventional devices and employing fresh ones instead.

As the Writer finishes with Manasi, our attention is drawn towards four late-comers in the theatre looking for their seats. The Writer addresses them directly asking them on the stage. Besides audience involvement, there is simulation of 'interruption' here *a la* Brecht.[5] Suggestive of a sense of urgency and participation, it also points to the Writer's search for *dramatis personae* about whom he could write a play—a contrived reversal of Pirandello's *Six Characters in Search of an Author*. Also it serves Badal Sircar's purpose in locating how things have changed, changed utterly, and a terrible truth is born. Owing to the suddenness of change, there is a pervasive bewilderment. Perhaps, this is a global phenomenon, as after the World War II the world began contracting fast. What Arthur Miller records in the Introduction to his *Collected Plays* is singularly opposite: "It was as though the whole country had been born anew, without a memory even of certain elemental decencies which a year or two earlier no one would have imagined could be altered, let alone forgotten."[6] It was not a gradual development, but a sudden, shocking spurt having no regard for the past—immediate or distant. For the past generation, it was a new iconoclasm, for the present, it was *the* thing. Such a situation of conflict did not come from the outside, but was a result, as it were, of some psychic disturbance born of disillusionment.

Badal Sircar dramatizes the socio-psychological conflict consequent upon certain external forces. Amal, Vimal, Kamal and Indrajit (the four whom the Writer called on the stage) are individuals, representatives and types all in one. The problem they face is perhaps, a nameless one, or that they are incapable of pronouncing it. They feel, they suffer, but they cannot enunciate. Worse still, the Writer, who is Greek chorus, Indian Sutradhar, and the Shakespearean fool rolled into one, has hardly any answer to socio-economic and moral crises. *Evam Indrajit* is a sad commentary on a change that was not opted for but thrust upon.

Yet a very significant characteristic of the play is its covert insistence on change. As a result, here in a different set-up, the concept of dramaturgy (with particular reference to Indian theatre) undergoes a change. An amalgam of conventionality and novelty—an evidence of change—is the very basis of the play. There lies its difficulty as well as its interest: this is dramatization of what's difficult (or, as Yeats would put it 'the fascination of what's difficult').[7] Unsuccessful in his love for Manasi, Indrajit takes recourse to the set notion of committing suicide. But Hamlet-like he finds himself a prisoner of indecision. The playwright shows that he lives more in thought than in action. Because he is truly modern so he is a lonely person.[8] Hence he is incomprehensible to the ordinary man; he is a shade different from Amal, Vimal and

Kamal. Sircar makes clear at the outset that the play is about the educated urban middle-class. Addressing the audience, the Writer says that according to the census of 1961 the population of Calcutta is nearly three crores, two-and-a-half percent of it being graduates. (6) Indrajit belongs to this group yet he is different. While the Writer pronounces the names of others in one breath, he pauses before uttering 'Indrajit' indicating, paradoxically, his alienation from the group as well as an alienation from the self.

Thereafter there is the first exposure of the audience to the technique of transformation. The same characters play the roles of college students and teachers. Such a technique presupposes the audience's knowledge that the world of drama is one of make-believe. Further, it also assures its participation and involvement. The playwright takes this opportunity of commenting on these characters suggesting that one person is many person having several facets to one's personality: "As you all know, different conditions, different cultures, different countries have produced plays about Indrajit and Manasi." (6)

Sircar is not only writing a new sort of play, but he is theorizing too. The distinction between the playwright and the audience breaks down for it is an intellectual exercise based on the idea of participation. Sharad Joshi employs a similar device in *Andhon ka Hathi* (The Blindmen's Elephant), and Vijay Tendulkar in *Shantata: Court Chalu Ahe* (Silence: The Court is in Session) uses the technique of transformation and role-changing not only externally but also psychologically. In fact, change is writ large in the construction of *Evam Indrajit* besides its focus on social change.

All the three acts of the play end with the words of the Writer: the first two having only the Writer whereas the last one has a chorus of voices. Not variation, but monotony appears to be the staple of life. So gyration becomes a very important image, perhaps the central image, in *Evam Indrajit*. Our life is a ritual of gyration, whose significance eludes us and most of us do not even bother to question why we do what we do. Perhaps, one tries to follow the path of the least resistance. A dialogue between Manasi and Indrajit in the first Act (21) brings the point home. They talk of rules of life. These rules relate to *rite de passage* as it were. Indrajit accepts certain rules, but his psyche revolts; he wants to bring down all the walls that fetter him but he is no Samson. So he gets into a foolish fit of fury. To Manasi he honestly accepts that he is fighting "The world! The people around us! What you call society." (22) An individual of Indrajit's calibre cannot change the society and so he falls a prey to impotent anger. Yet Sircar's intention is clear as daylight: he is writing for a social change that will usher in, if not a better order, at least, a new one shorn of the monotony of familiarity.

Yet dissatisfaction prolongs its shadow over all earth-bound men and women who have become voyeurs in their own drama. The Writer's declamation, at the end of the first act, is tinged with sadness inherent in human life itself. "More atoms, many more atoms, mix and mingle and make up the ferris wheel of this giant earth that goes round and round," (29) as it points to man's puny helplessness. It may seem that the play dramatizes the meaningless existence of the middle-class, but in fact, it is a sardonic comment on the monotony and boredom of life, yet an undercurrent of change is discernible. Manasi's and Indrajit's acceptance of the *rules* is not the same thing: the former accepts without qualification whereas Indrajit's has revolt latent in it. The truth is told, the sordidness of life surfaces, ennui is broadcast, petulant anger disturbs, but the playwright does not let go the hold.

Sircar employs puppetry and mimicry: "The entire interview is mimed," (28) and again, "Amal, Vimal and Kamal take on appropriate voices and gestures although there is a hint of puppet-show in their movements." (7) Modernism, then, does not consist in breaking away from tradition, but by accepting the past, it transcends it through transformation. *Evam Indrajit* is a case in point. Employment of various techniques has hybridized the form. To my mind, this hybridization is an experiment with novelty representing simultaneously a change in socio-cultural ethos. As the 'difficulty' or 'obscurity' of modern poetry was the result of an effort at fnding proper expression for the fractured self of the modern man, so, of necessity, modern drama requires a fresh mode of expression. Clinging to convention would be of hardly any help. Moreover, social awareness makes it obligatory for the playwright to seek a new approach and exposure.

Evam Indrajit narrates the ordinary, the everyday; portrays the routine of life (36-38) and the repetitive comment of the Writer adds to the monotony and disillusionment. In this changed set-up, adjustments are difficult. The *dramatis personae* are those who have failed to adjust themselves (for they refuse to compromise) and the Writer as a ubiquitous presence probes the lives of Amal, Vimal, Kamal and Indrajit in their various roles as educated unemployed young men to successful persons in their respective fields, to students, to teachers, to husbands, to fathers and to many more parts they have to play: an individual, after all, is a many splendoured object. Sircar gives a new turn to the Shakespeare imagery of 'world stage,' and the symbols of gyration, of search, of fruitless repetitiveness seem to have descended from, among others, Yeats and Eliot. Indeed, in spite of its masked dependence on Ibsen, Shaw, Pirandello and Brecht, *Evam Indrajit* is clearly a new play so far as the Indian theatre scene is concerned.

The invocation of the Sisyphus image towards the end of the play appears inevitable. After so much of dramatization of the pointlessness of the middle-class existence, Sircar does not throw up his hands in despair. Disillusionment is not always enervating. Instead of cynicism, he emphasizes the Sisyphean effort even if the rock rolls down time and again. Social conventions have to be pushed out, for man cannot live a monotonous life for ever. Whether or not the change would usher in a better social order is a moot point, but unbearable, suffocating societal norms are not to be suffered interminably. The *leit motif* of human life being quest, the effort has to continue.

Perhaps, *Evam Indrajit* will not bring in the desired change yet it may lead us to critical thinking. It is a disturbing play having shaken the audience (society) from its cozy stupor. Clash of interests and anti-establishmentarianism inspire Sircar to promote social change through drama, the most influential artistic vehicle to ride the bandwagon of progress and development. Hence the *dramatis personae* are everyman, the incidents dramatized are everyday. The ritualistic emphasis on monotony and disillusionment deftly indicates the need for a social change. The play, therefore, becomes both an instrument of change and the product of change itself.

Such a commitment to change comes out of a passionate faith in human progress and shows an indignation in the acceptance of worn out values in their drabness. The rock, after all, may be overturned for the flesh may be weak, but the spirit is indomitable.

NOTES

1. G.J. Watson, *Drama: An Introduction* (New York: St. Martin's Press, 1983), p. 2.
2. W.B. Yeats, *The Collected Poems* (London: Macmillan, 1955), p. 401.
3. *The Complete Prefaces* (London: Paul Hamlyn, 1965), p. 729.
4. Badal Sircar, *Evam Indrajit* (Calcutta: O.U.P., 1985).
5. Bertlot Brecht, *Poems: Part Two* (London: Eyre Methuen, 1976), p. 178.
6. (New York: The Viking Press, 1987), Vol. I, p. 40.
7. Yeats, p. 104.
8. C.G. Jung, *Modern Man in Search of a Soul* (London: Routledge and Kegan Paul, 1962), p. 227.

Dionysian Ego in Girish Karnad's *Hayavadana*

MANCHI SARAT BABU

Norman O. Brown, a psychoanalyst, uses the Greek myths of Apollo and Dionysus in interpreting the alienation of mind and body and their unification.[1] According to psychoanalysis, human mind is divided into three organs; the id, the ego and the superego. The id consists of instinctual drives and always seeks gratification irrespective of external reality and cultural values (Pleasure principle). The ego perceives and responds to external reality (Reality principle). It, being the leader, tries to satisfy the id and the superego within the limits of external reality. The superego irrespective of external reality and biological impulses (the id) contains ideals, values and morals and urges the ego to lead an ideal life. When the ego wants to be ideal under the pressure of the superego, the mind starts functioning independent of the body. This naturally leads to a split between the mind and the body. Consequently they become strangers to each other. That is, the experiences of the body do not reach the mind and the feelings of the mind do not spread through the body. Such an ego as causes this self-alienation is called Apollonian ego in which the soul leaves the body as Brown puts it. On the other hand when the ego wants to be natural or really human and when the superego accepts the biological reality (the id), the mind and the body work together. There is no split between them. There is perfect harmony between them. The mind feels the bodily experiences and the body rocks with the feelings of the mind. This is what Blake describes as 'the undivided body-soul.' Such an ego as allows the undifferentiated, unified body-mind is called Dionysian ego in which the soul returns to and resides in, the body as Brown explains.

According to psychoanalytical interpretation of history as expounded by Brown, human history is divided into three phases; primal unity, differentiation and final unity. The primitive man enjoyed the primal unity of the body and the mind. As man civilizes himself through ages, the body and the mind are differentiated, divided and finally alienated. All human suffering is only due to this culture of self-alienation (Apollonian Culture). When the intense suffering brings about awareness, man stops feeling ashamed of being human. As human knowledge reaches its zenith, he evolves Dionysian culture through which he retains the undifferentiated unified mind-body. This final unity is the salvation that the future human society attains according to the optimistic prediction of psychoanalysis. This concept helps us solve such riddles in *Hayavadana* as why Hayavadana's mother chooses for her husband a stallion rather than a man and why Goddess Kali makes Hayavadana a complete horse instead of a complete man.

The theme of *Hayavadana*[2] is the problem of alienation rather than 'incompleteness' which in the play means alienation as we are going to see. The play starts with the worship and then the description of Lord Ganesha, the elephant-headed god, who symbolizes alienation since his head and his body are incompatible. A little later Hayavadana, the eponymous character, comes and like Ganesha he too is a symbol of alienation since he is a horse-headed man. Karnad makes use of these mythical figures to throw light on the alienation of man and its consequences in human society. He tries to show suggestively the hegemony of Apollonian culture that has captured the racial unconscious of mankind. The modern man represented by Devadatta-Kapila suffers from self-alienation. Goddess Kali's power proves to be very weak since the transposition of their heads fails to liberate Devadatta and Kapila from alienation.

> Padmini: Must the head always win?
> Kapila: That's why I am Kapila now. (56)

It is the hegemonistic culture which wins through the head. Devadatta discontinues physical exercise and gradually loses his physical vigour while Kapila regains his physical vigour by taking rigorous physical exercise. This is because the cultural roles of Devadatta, a brahmin and Kapila, a blacksmith, carried in their heads respectively, successfully undo what is granted by Goddess Kali.

> Devadatta: All the muscle and strength. But how long can one go on like that? I have the family tradition to maintain—the daily reading, writing and studies. (46)

Devadatta is a brahmin. He reads and writes. He develops his mind and ignores his body. Kapila is a blacksmith. He is adept in making and repairing carts and other things. He plays games and participates in sports. He develops his body and neglects his mind. While describing their friendship, Bhagavata says "one mind, one heart." Devadatta is "the mind" and Kapila is "the heart." Actually their friendship is based on the fact that they depend on each other for what each lacks. That is why Raykar says, "They are thus complementary to each other."[3] Since the mind is considered superior to the body in human society, the caste of Brahmins occupies a higher rung than all other castes in our hierarchical society. That is why Devadatta sits on a chair while Kapila squats on the floor. Since real love is not possible between two inequal persons, their friendship is not real. The dishonesty of their friendship is well exposed by Goddess Kali. "Kali . . . says he is dying for friendship. He must have known perfectly well he would be accused of killing Devadatta for you." (33) The covert conflict between Devadatta and Kapila which comes out after the transposition of their heads stands for the antagonism of human mind and body. It culminates in the duel that kills them both. This shows that alienation is lethal to both the mind and the body.

Devadatta is 'the mind' and Kapila 'the body.' Devadatta falls in love fifteen times in a period of two years. (12) Yet he fails to get married to any one of the girls. Even his sixteenth love seems to be a fiasco. He feels utterly hopeless and helpless: "I swear, Kapila, with you as my witness I swear, if I ever get her as my wife, I'll sacrifice my two arms to the goddess Kali, I'll sacrifice my head to Lord Rudra." (14) Unlike Devadatta, Kapila does not fall in love. He does not feel it difficult to arrange the marriage of Devadatta and Padmini. Devadatta's body does not respond as adequately as his mind readily loves and Kapila's mind is not nimble enough to feel the sensations of his body. Thus both suffer from self-alienation. Therefore the problem is more than the passiveness of Devadatta's body and Kapila's mind. There is little or no communication between their body and mind. Padmini, not realizing the real problem, juxtaposes the active mind (head) of Devadatta and the active body of Kapila. So, even after the transposition of their heads, their self-alienation continues since each head carries deep in itself the Apollonian ego.

The alienation of the mind and the body is unnatural and artificial while their unification is natural. Apollonian culture strives for alienation while nature seeks unification. Libido (life impulses) of Freud or the Life Force of Bernard Shaw tirelessly tries to bring about, unification. It can be seen functioning through Hayavadana's mother (the princess of Karnataka) and Padmini. The Princess therefore prefers a stallion to a human prince because animals are free from alienation. When the stallion becomes a gandharva after fifteen years, she requests him to remain a horse. She does not regret her becoming a mare when the enraged gandharva curses her. As Hayavadana says: "He cursed her to become a horse herself. So my mother became a horse and ran away happily." (9) The stallion's becoming the gandharva symbolizes the primitive man's becoming the civilized man. Mother Kali also favours nature. She therefore grants Hayavadana's wish to become complete. He becomes a complete horse instead of a complete man. By doing so, the Goddess liberates Hayavadana from self-alienation. Thus Hayavadana as well as his mother attains Dionysian ego.

Padmini fails to achieve the reunification of the mind and the body in Devadatta-Kapila. She realizes her mistake and perceives the real problem. She explains the problem to Kapila whose mind is frigid to the sensations of his body on account of self-alienation:

> Be quiet, stupid. Your body bathed in a river, swam and danced in it. Shouldn't your head know what river it was, what swim? Your head too must submerge in that river—the flow must rumple your hair, run its tongue in your ears and press your head to its bosom! Until that's done, you'll continue to be incomplete. (58)

She wants to achieve her aim through her son. So she requests the Bhagavata to let her son be brought up as the son of Kapila by the hunters in the forest for five years and then as the son of Devadatta by Vidyasagara, her father-in-law and learned brahmin. Thus she wants to provide both physical and mental training for her son so that he may attain unification. After passing her oral will to the Bhagavata, she commits sati on the pyre of Devadatta and Kapila who have died in a duel. Thus she ends her life of alienation and averts the possible dilution of her will.

Padmini's son is brought to the Bhagavata again after five years. He is as morose as Kapila after his transposition. Hayavadana who becomes a complete horse comes and expresses his grief over his human voice. When he laughs with human voice, Padmini's son throws away his dolls and starts laughing and clapping as if he were freed from a spell. Similarly Hayavadana loses human voice when Padmini's son rides him and sings a nursery rhyme. Thus Hayavadana and Padmini's son symbolizing the primal unity and the final unity respectively attain Dionysian ego. Padmini thus succeeds in achieving her aim posthumously. As Bhagavata says: "So at last Hayavadana has become complete. (To the Actors) You two go and tell the Revered Brahmin

Vidyasagar that his grandson is returning home in triumph, riding a big, white charge." (71) Padmini's son representing the future man achieves harmony not only between the mind and the body but also between himself and nature represented by Hayavadana.

Most of the critics including M.K. Naik[4] and Shubhangi S. Raykar think that it is humanly impossible to achieve perfection. Raykar in her brilliant paper on *Hayavadana* argues that the unification of Apollo and Dionysus symbolized by Devadatta and Kapila is not all possible. This present study being based on psychoanalysis is entirely different from the earlier ones of *Hayavadana*. In the primitive man, the body and the mind are in perfect harmony which Brown calls Dionysian ego. As man has been vainly striving to be above biological principles for ages, he has evolved Apollonian culture which causes alienation. Devadatta and Kapila like the people of modern society are the victims of self-alienation while Hayavadana, his mother and Padmini's son attain Dionysian ego (the undifferentiated body-mind).

NOTES

1. Norman O. Brown, "Apollo and Dionysus," *Life against Death* (London: Routledge and Kegan Paul, 1959), pp. 155-76.
2. Girish Karnad, *Hayavadana* (New Delhi: Oxford University Press, 1988).
3. Shubhangi S. Raykar, "The Development of Girish Karnad as a Dramatist: *Hayavadana*," *Studies in Contemporary Indian Drama*, ed. Sudhakar Pandey and Freya Taraporewala (New Delhi: Prestige, 1990), p. 50.
4. M.K. Naik, "From the Horse Mouth: A Study of *Hayavadana*" *Dimensions of Indian English Literature* (New Delhi: Sterling, 1984), pp. 191-201.

An Authentic Voice of the Theatre: A Tribute to Asif Currimbhoy

M. PUSHPA

Asif Currimbhoy's sudden death on 1 June 1994 left all his admirers stunned. A man who was a keen student of life and the theatre just disappeared from the scenario of life. Though my knowledge of his genius may not be very wide, yet I would like to pay a small tribute to this great dramatist on the occasion of his first death anniversary.

Asif Currimbhoy was a writer who made a significant contribution to the Indian theatre. Many of us, perhaps, were not fully aware of his abilities. Born in a distinguished Khoja family in Bombay he was exposed to the Western culture through education. His wife Suraiya was a great source of inspiration to him. His plays include *The Tourist Mecca, Doldrummers, Goa, This Alien . . . Native Land, Inquilab, The Refugee, Sonar Bangla, The Dumb Dancer, Thorns on a Canvas, The Hungry Ones*. These plays display a variegated background and themes. Human interest and social realism are two significant props of his dramatic constructions.

Love from time immemorial has been the leitmotif of many works of literature. Currimbhoy understood the value of love and of man's inner urge to find meaning in life through love. The irony is that love sometimes instead of being a sustaining force becomes a tragic flaw. Love, nevertheless, is the immediate need of man, for a lack of it leads to many maladies of the post-modern era. Love in the form of sex can be misused. It calls for adjustment, and if people are not ready for it, it leads to tragedy. In *Tourist Mecca* the young Keshav Singh is lost in contemplation. One Janet Toppin from a group of tourists, falls in love with him. Thus love runs into rough weather as the mother lays an obstacle on the path. Keshav is non-plussed at her decision. This love runs into rough weather as the mother lays an obstacle on the path. Keshav is non-plussed at her decision. This play was Currimbhoy's first play, but technically it was a compact one. The title explains to us the conflict between reality and dream. Taj Mahal is a monument dedicated to true love, but now it exists only in dream.

The *Doldrummers* as a play explores the hollowness of life. Ruth, Tony, Joe and Liza reflect the element of irony in life. They are all in a blind alley as it were, devoid of a sense of responsibility. These characters are all schizophrenics who have created a smug little world. They struggle to give meaning to their lives, but do not succeed. These dejected young men and women are very much products of our culture. They are segments of this world of actuality.

Man, when in conflict, uses violence as a weapon to fight against odds. *Goa* is a play which deals with love between Kishore and Rita, Alphonso and Rose. This simple story develops into a strange play of deep emotions and uncontrollable forces. The love plot seems to run parallel to the political sub-plot. The play suggests that whatever is remote and unreal is mysterious. Man resorts to brutality only when he is helpless. Love sometimes has a withdrawn effect. It is like the waves which come in fast and disappear in that manner. It can be devastating in its effects. As a writer summed up the tragic quality of love in general, "Love thrives in proximity but dies on contact."

Currimbhoy keeps track of the modern problems. The most pressing problem is power. Man clamours for power not for constructive purposes but to destroy the world. It is not combined with a renunciation of self. Power seekers are there everywhere in the world. Political leaders exploit the youth and the students. In *Inquilab* Currimbhoy remarks: "Youth . . . an youth is like . . . the overripe mango . . . feed it too much and it falls!" Young people, the pillars of tomorrow, crumble today under the load of diffidence. *Inquilab* is not a revolution through violence but by the exercise of free will. Prof. Datta in this play is a follower of non-violence. The son Aman is against the father and is a revolutionist. Students are inexperienced and they are led astray by the political barons. The leaders use political intentions as a facade to gain their own ends. Shomik is a leader who wants liberation through revolution. Basically a peasant, he decides to furrow the land with fierceness. He acts like a tyrant. Currimbhoy encourages democracy as revolution.

The tragedy of war is the theme of *The Refugee*. Deeply disturbed by the refugees who poured in from Bangladesh, Currimbhoy was prompted to explore "the predicament of humanity caught in the political restlessness, moral mooring and psychological alienation." The protagonist here is dejected and is constantly nagged by the thought of his status as a refugee. He is shell-shocked as it were and goes about in a trance-like state. A very valid point is made by Currimbhoy. Refugees soon become burdens; their salvation lies not in seeking protection in some other land, but fighting for their rights at home. Refugees are exploited by powerseekers and transform into anti-social elements.

Playwrights like Sircar, Girish Karnad and Asif Currimbhoy are concerned with the role of man in society. Their plays are a reflection of man's hopes and fears, faith and doubts. It is a social morality which gives identity to human beings. Reality and illusion are two distinct worlds—there is always a conflict between them. *The Dumb Dancer* dramatizes man's need for belonging that is, his sense of identification. Sanity is a thin dividing line between the real world and the unreal world. The real world is a make-believe world where one has split personality, but in the unreal world the person identifies himself with the make-believe. Life is a maze and every man spends his time trying to read this mystery.

Currimbhoy was a prolific writer. He wrote plays for the sheer pleasure of expressing his ideas and observations. His plays are multicoloured intricately woven designs. No specific label can be given to his plays. Love in its many splendoured form is depicted in plays like *The Tourist Mecca, Goa, This Alien . . . Native Land.* War is an event which creates ripples in the placid lives of the people. Plays like *The Hungry Ones* and *Thorns on a Canvas* are portraits of social realism. People should learn to live together, respect each other's feelings and beliefs.

Asif Currimbhoy presents a variety of experiences from different angles. His deft handling of language and his choice of simple themes are the main props of his plays. Love and compassion are the buoys which help people to keep afloat in this sea of torment and pain, of worldliness and mental anguish. A Karmayogi, the authentic voice of the theatre, a forceful playwright are some of the terms used to describe the forceful personality of Currimbhoy. Above all he was an optimist. He said: "Everyone dreams. That's hoping and everyone must hope."

R.K. Narayan and Manohar Malgonkar: A Study in Artistic Escape into the Past

I. VENKATEŚWARLU

The Indian English novelists had cashed heavily on anti-imperialistic platform where the ugly villain was the British raj. They could find selfless leaders like Mahatma Gandhi, who were a source of inspiration for them to make their novels reach Himalayan heights. The then leaders could awake mass-consciousness in the minds of the people and create a sense of unity by raising their finger at the British raj.

But after independence the novelists found themselves almost lost because the traditional villain against whom they could rouse the feelings of public is no more. They were in a fix, unable to understand who should be treated as a villain in the changed circumstances. But imaginative powers of the novelists are not kept in cold storage. They struggled to find a way out to manifest the novelist's imaginative powers. K. Srinivasa Iyengar says that these novelists, in the changed circumstances, are apt either to turn in nostalgia to the past and glorify and idealize it or to turn to the present in a gesture of protest if not disgust. What Iyengar says is proved right by R.K. Narayan and Manohar Malgonkar. Both of them in their post-independence fiction begin to look back to the past and glorify whatever they found. They also did not hesitate to show their protest against the shortcomings in the post-independence scenario. Through his ironic mode R.K. Narayan has made fun of a number of things which he thinks are out of moral orbit. But Manohar Malgonkar has gone to extreme ends of the protest by spitting venom on unethical situations in the modern society after independence. Both these novelists in their own way tried to escape the modern realities. Sometimes they take up historical fiction in order to idealize the past situation and at other times they enter into a kind of sentimental romantic situation in their fictional outputs. Thus both can be charged with the guilt of escapism. But by virtue of their gifted powers of writing they could make a mark in their own way, whatever they attempted.

R.K. Narayan's *The Dark Room* (1938) though a pre-independence novel, has all the trappings of a post-independence fiction. Here the writer combines tradition with modernity. The story is more traditional in several ways. The protagonist Savitri betrays epical dimensions. The Savitri of the myth was different from Narayan's Savitri. The mythical character was a devoted wife who could prove her sterling qualities of wife to bring back the life of her husband from the hands of the God of Death itself. She never felt that she was living in a male-dominated society at the mercy of her man. But she was not happy when she was left alone after the sudden death of her husband. In a way loneliness was unbearable to her. The deep-rooted tradition testifies to this fact. R.K. Narayan's Savitri has a hellish experience outside her home. Finally she has to come back and make compromise with her husband at least for the sake of her children. However bad her husband may be, she regains her old equilibrium in her domestic environment. Here R.K. Narayan tries to glorify the notion of wife's devotion to her husband.

In *The Financial Expert* (1952) again, the writer tries to bring both traditional and modern outlooks at cross-roads and finally votes for the victory of the traditional notion. In *The Guide* also, the writer tries to prove the idea of a swami, in traditional terms who can be exploited to the extent of transforming a lie into a truth. Such a theme potentially finds favour with the people who are preoccupied, since the times immemorial, with spiritual notions of *sanyasis* and *sadhus* doing good to society. In R.K. Narayan's literary output names change, fashions change, but the soul of the place is unalterably itself. The old landmarks in Malgudi—the Sarayu, the hills, the jungles, the grove, remain, defying the onslaught of change. Here again the novelist takes shelter in the traditional universals, to sustain a lively interest in his fictional mode. The disappointed lover of *The Bachelor of Arts* becomes a *sadhu* for a change—*sanyasi, swami and Mahatma* are names that can cover many sins and describe many virtues if one is prepared to think of them in terms of Indian traditional way of life.

In brief R.K. Narayan presents human nature interestingly and memorably without any overt condemnation or praise. This is mainly because the traditional past of R.K. Narayan makes him so much detached from human being and the way of life. As a matter of fact, it is difficult to say that R.K. Narayan's characters are good or bad. It is this element of detachment which enriches the traditional overtones of his artistic presentation. In his novels there is generally a flight, an uprooting, a disturbance of order—followed by a return, renewal, a restoration of normalcy.

This kind of form has the touch of the Indian traditions. Despite the writer's small talk, the miracle of faith plays a crucial role in R.K. Narayan's fiction.

Manohar Malgonkar stands an equal to R.K. Narayan in his traditional outlook. His *Distant Drum* (1960) and *A Bend in the Ganges* (1964) constitute no mean achievement. In *Distant Drum*, the writer probes deep into the aspects of army life which is depicted in all its glory. Kiran Garud is a symbol of army life and its code of conduct. The novelist instills a sense of happy association and liking for the army life in the minds of the readers. His protest for the existing evils in society takes the form of disgust which he never ever tried to hide in his novels. The red-tapism, nepotism, casteism are all soul-killing evils in modern India. Malgonkar never spared condemning these shortcomings in his characters. In his novels, if the army officer stands for certain positive qualities, the political boss typifies the opposite qualities. To Malgonkar, the political leaders pulling strings from far away are the shame of the nation. Thus the writer's protest is revealed in the form of disgust.

Combat of Shadows (1962) illustrates the epigraph from the *Gita*: "Desire and Aversion are opposite shadows." The spiritual overtones are neatly embedded in the novel. Like R.K. Narayan, Manohar Malgonkar also idealizes the tractional notions. Henry Weinton and Eddie Trevor are a fine contrast. They make love to each other's beloveds. Desire is the root cause of all troubles in life. This desire in the form of consuming love has destroyed them towards the end of the novel. Desire in the initial stages leading to aversion at the final stages is beautifully and neatly illustrated in the novel through the two pairs of lovers: Henry Winton and Ruby Miranda, Eddie Trevor and Jean Walters. It is a strange complication making aversion the dominant element in the story. At the end one has the feeling that poetic justice is done because Henry Winton dies a miserable death with the clear knowledge that Ruby, Pasupati and Dart have together brought the terrible punishment of death on him.

His another novel *The Princes* (1963) also illustrates how the writer has given vent to his desire to escape into India of pre-independence days. He found that the past glorious days are more charming and honest than the present. The very fact that the place of the Maharaja was taken cunningly by upstart politicians has a revolting sense, breeding dislike and disgust. The writer has succeeded in making the people cast their eyes nostalgically back to the days that are no more. This is true of the novels of both R.K. Narayan and Manohar Malgonkar.

The Heart is a Lonely Hunter: R.K. Narayan's Rosie turned Nalini

A.K. MUKHERJEE

"A profound unmitigated loneliness is the only truth of life" is what Narayan says in *The English Teacher*. It is also true of *The Guide*, much-talked-of novel of Narayan. And the lonely character of the novel is Rosie who is changed into Nalini for purposes of publicity, she becomes a sex symbol like Marilyn Monroe, sought after by the public, exploited by Raju, the hero of the novel. The fate of the novel is that it has always been discussed with reference to the character of Raju who is forced to be a saint from a self-styled tourist guide. Raju, the imposter plays his role well and ultimately falls a prey to his own making. But Rosie, the dancer, committed to her own art suffers in loneliness when she sees her faith in art thwarted by a man to whom she had turned after being spurned by her own husband. *The Guide* is not only the story of Raju; it is also the story about the plight of an artist amidst philistines. She is the lonely hunter, hunting for a meaning to her life.

This paper does not aim at vindicating the cause of feminism but it will make an analysis of the novel from a humanist point of view, without inclining to any warring group: male chauvinism or feminism.

The problem with R.K. Narayan is his language which is too simple and at the same time too ironical to be understood by the Indian readers who like Narayan's Velan refuse to take words without any connotative attributes attached to them. The Indian reader is another Sherlock Holmes who is always in search of some metaphysical significance to anything spoken by a writer. This is, perhaps, the reason why foreigners look at Indians, mostly writers, with awe and astonishment. R.K. Narayan very neatly presents his predicament at Harvard in his essay "Reluctant Guru."

It is also the plight of the novel *The Guide*. The novel has been studied as the story of the Railway Raju, a guide, turned into a saint by circumstances. What the critics have overlooked in their readings of the novel is the story of an artist, Rosie, the dancer in a male-dominated society.

A daughter of a devdasi, Rosie could not sever her connection with her traditional art. A devdasi is supposed to be a dancer before God. She offers herself to God and remains his mistress. Besides being trained in the traditional art of her family, Rosie was an M.A. in Economics, and her mother wanted her to lead a decent life, different from her own life by marrying an educated man. But it is difficult for a devdasi to find in the Indian society a groom for her daughter. Marco married Rosie when he found in her a woman satisfying all the qualities as advertised by him in a newspaper.

Their marriage failed since Marco and Rosie were diametrically opposite in nature. Macro belonged to a dead world. He was a historian, deeply engaged in his research work inside the caves. He came to Malgudi not as a tourist, but as a historian to read the sculptures of her caves, to collect materials for his book on Malgudi. But his wife Rosie accompanied him as a tourist who wanted to see the beautiful sights of Malgudi, the snake dance; her caves were myths of delight to her because of their unfathomable darkness and mystery. She was an artist, a born dancer, desired to cultivate her interest in dancing. She wished to reach perfection in Bharat Natyam. She was a being of the living world; she was hungry for the warmth, love from her husband. Marco was cold, both sexually and mentally. A cold stone wall could excite him much more than a living body of a beautiful woman. When Raju asked her about her interest she said, "Anything except cold, old stone walls." (83) Marco once said to Raju, "If a man has to have peace of mind it is best that he forget the fair sex." (71) Their wide difference is well remarked by Rosie, "When we are all alone and start talking, we argue and quarrel over everything. We don't argue on most matters, and then he leaves me alone and comes back and we are all right, that's all." (83)

Rosie is an artist who wants to live every moment of her life. Everything allures her to live intensely. Their stay in the peak house on the topmost cliff on Mempi Hills lifts her spirit. She runs like a child from plant to plant with joy while Marco sits without any emotion. Raju remarks, "Anything that interested her seemed to irritate him." (76)

An artist needs appreciation—a sympathetic understanding of his or her creation. Rosie loves dancing. In her first meeting with Raju, the latter asks her to show him the dance of a cobra. Marco calls her interest "morbid." (84) When she begs him to permit her to dance, "I think I'd like to try. Just as you are trying to—." Marco retorts, "Oh, you want to rival me, is that it? This is a branch of learning, not street acrobatics." (147) Dance, thus, was not an art for him but "street acrobatics." This unkind and unsympathetic attitude of her husband made her life miserable. She felt suffocated and was trying to find an outlet. The outlet was opened by the arrival of Raju in her life. Raju was an intelligent and cunning tourist guide. He could see the rift between the wife and the husband. He could also read the mind of Rosie: "She liked to loaf in the market, eat in a crowded hotel, wander about, see a cinema—these common pleasures seemed to have been beyond her reach all these days." (58) He won her confidence when he took her to show the dance of a king cobra. Raju was astonished when he saw her dancing in the street with the dance of the king cobra. It was a revelation to Raju. He encouraged her to dance. He came closer to her; he won her. She got what she had not got from her husband. Their deep intimacy led to her separation from her husband. She thought she had found a man who understood her; who would make her dreams a reality; who would fulfil her desire as a woman and as an artist: "She brightened up. Her eyes lit up with a new fervour at the mention of dancing. So I sat up with her, helping her to day-dream. I found out the clue to her affection and utilized it to the utmost. Her art and her husband could not find a place in her thoughts at the same time; one drove the other out." (122) She started her daily practice in the morning before a bronze figure and in the forenoon studied the theory, *Natya Shastra* of Bharat Muni. A pandit was engaged to teach her Sanskrit. She forgot the world around her and was fully wedded to her art. She strove for perfection.

But her disillusionment began when she found Raju exploiting her art for their material prosperity. She was forced to give her performance every evening without any respite. Rosie was changed into Nalini for more popularity; the name Nalini sounded Indian, it sounded more beautiful; more sonorous to the ears. People booked in advance to see her dance. Rocket like, she soared. This hectic, busy life tired her soon. She had not expected Raju to use her like bull "yoked to an oil-crusher" who is to "go round and round, in a circle, without a beginning or an end." (202) She told her plight to Raju, "I feel like one of those parrots in a cage taken around village fairs, or a performing monkey." (203) She had not expected her art to be commercialized; she did not want her performance to be staged before the philistines who came to look at her beautiful body, and not to understand her art. She once commented on her audience: "They might be logs of wood for all I care. When I dance I hardly notice any face. I just see a dark wall in the auditorium, that's all." (211) She danced because she loved it. It was her passion. The word dance stung Marco; Raju used it to make his fortune. She hardly found any difference between Marco and Raju. One tortured her physically and emotionally while the other tortured her spiritually. Dance was, for Rosie, a kind of spiritual exercise. That was why she could not totally forget Marco. Raju appeared as selfish as Marco. For both of them a woman is a commodity to be used; if you dislike it, ignore it or throw it away. It became more evident to her when Raju was exposed with his meanness. He was imprisoned for committing forgery. He betrayed Rosie by hiding the book given to her by her husband. Raju appeared small before her. She felt lost, the firm ground under her feet seemed to be slithering. When Raju implored her to dance, in spite of their misfortune, she firmly retorted: "Even if you are free, I'll not dance in public any more. I am tired of all this circus existence." (221)

She wanted to live alone, left to herself. She needed freedom to be herself which was denied to her by her husband, and lover too. She said to Raju, "If I have to pawn my last possession, I'll do it to save you from jail. But, once it is over, leave me alone once and for all; that's all I ask. Forget me. Leave me to live or die as I choose; that's all." (221-22)

Rosie was a lonely heart hunting for a meaning to her existence. Male-dominated society failed to hold a meaning to her existence; it betrayed her. She at last, returned to her art. Art, at least, will not leave her in despair.

This theme in the novel is covered by Raju's appearance in Mangalpur, and the role of Velan to make him a saint. R.K. Narayan, perhaps, wanted to expose the hypocrisy and deceit of Raju. As black takes no other hue, the imprisonment could not bring about any change in Raju. He was rather more fortified in Mangalpur. But he is entrapped in his own trap; he came to believe in his own role. The novelist laughs at Raju, the people of Mangalpur, and the world at large. The people, mostly, are credulous. In spite of everything, the world has not progressed much. Man still believes that fasting can bring rain. It is not spiritualism, rather charlatanism. It is the fear of God that makes each one of us cling to false gods or godmen. Narayan laughs at this attitude of man. It is evident from his use of language, his tone, and his narrative pattern. Art has no meaning in this world. We never love it; we admire it; we use it for our own ends. Rosie turned Nalini has no room in this world where "flesh, fish or fowl, commend all summer long." (Yeats, "Sailing to Byzantium") Her story, therefore, takes a back seat in the novel. But one thing is sure that Raju fails to conquer or destroy the world of Nalini, the world of art. Rosie, like every true artist, is bound to return to her own self. Her heart is a lonely hunter.

Raja Rao's *The Serpent and the Rope*: The East-West Cocktail

SWARAJ KISHEN TIKOO

In *The Serpent and the Rope*,[1] as Paul Sharrad thinks,[2] Raja Rao promotes the view that after marriage Indians desire a son (rather than a daughter) first because he becomes a 'heir' and 'a lighter of the funeral fire' when his parents are cremated. It is true that the son performs the ritualistic role of the pyre-lighter which has become a centuries-old custom in Hindu society. This customary practice has resulted in a popular colloquialism that one should have a son to have at least a pyre-lighter. But to think of marriage in terms of merely a means of providing a 'heir' or a 'pyre-lighter' (233-34) is to belittle this human and social institution. This may not be construed as a full Indian view of marriage. If we think of the novel's great achievement in the field of Indian writing in English for the exposition of Indianness to both Indians as well as foreigners, then the light which it throws on the concept of marriage seems to be insufficient. In that sense it does not expound or present a complete Indian view of marriage. The desire for a son is universal because of the human desire for perpetuation supercedes the desire for son as a pyre-lighter. However, in the case of Indians the desire for a son is also a psychological and a social aspiration because of the prevalent patriarchal system[3] in which the son carries forward the family tradition because the daughter goes out of the family to stay in her husband's house. It is now an established practice that the daughter, who gets as much affection as the son in her father's house, is accorded a position only next to the son whenever the family's properties or responsibilities are shared. It owes to the widely recognized fact that during her pre-marital years the daughter is only a temporary member of the household. After her marriage she becomes a permanent member of her husband's household (except in certain communities in which the matriarchal system prevails whereby it is the son rather than the daughter who is married out of the mother's family). The firm adherence, conscious or unconscious, to this social practice has given rise to a popularly held view that the daughter after her marriage never returns to stay back in her father's house except in extreme circumstances when there is a mishap, or a calamity befalls her in her husband's house which may compel her separation from the husband and his family. There are innumerable newspaper reports of bride burning because the bride's parents fail to fulfil the high demands of dowry made by the husband's family. The brides languish in their husband's homes and silently suffer all kinds of tortures inflicted upon them by the husband's family because they cannot return to their parents' house for fear of being exposed to social contempt.

That the son is essentially desired by the parents not for being the pyre-lighter but because he would be the perpetuator of the family can be exemplified by yet another social practice of distribution of the family property. Most of the time all landed or immobile property is bestowed on the son while the daughter is given a dowry in marriage which she can conveniently carry along with her into the husband's house. Despite the social changes for the improvement of women's position that have come about in recent times and following verdicts of Indian courts giving sons and daughters an equal right to claim equally the property of the family and the wide publicity through visual and print media to promote the idea of their equality, the family practice of showing preference for the son over the daughter has not died down. The son is invariably expected to accept all obligations which may ensure continuity of the family and transmit its traditions to the future generations. In the light of this background to say that Rama's desire for a son is a desire for a pyre-lighter would be to misplace the emphasis on the situation in *The Serpent and the Rope*.

Arguing along this line Paul Sharrad interprets Rama's desire for a pyre-lighter as a 'death-wish.' This is a point on which one might differ with Sharrad. This view, if accepted, would characterize Indian view of life as negativistic and hence contrary to the commonly accepted view of life as a journey with a destination. Life, to an Indian generally, is a journey of love and romance which has ultimately a spiritual destination, the union with the divine. Indians also view life generally as a journey across an ocean, the successful crossing of which constitutes the salvation of the traveller. Our world on this shore of the ocean is regarded as 'maya' and the world beyond the ocean's end is visualized as nothing but divinity. Accordingly, after her marriage the daughter becomes the happy companion of her husband-traveller. The birth of children further brings happiness to the travellers and endows them with a greater drive towards achieving the noble purpose of completing the tasks set before them for arriving at their spiritual destination. This course of life, essentially grounded in the Vedas and the Upanishads, makes the Indian view of life ultimately wholesome and positivistic and not negativistic.[4] The philosophical dimensions of *The Serpent and the Rope* become manifest as the world and life are seen as "Maya" which is neither Illusion nor Reality but an intermediate state of Cosmic Illusion, a state which has its own concretized existence. It is from its concern with the philosophical theme that the novel has its title, *The Serpent and the Rope.* Both objects, the serpent and the rope, are real, but each deludes one into thinking of the other. The deception not only defies the sight but also sends a shudder down the spine.

Some of these fundamental facts bearing on the Indian view of life need unfailingly to be kept in mind when one analyzes Rama's character. Rama is an 'expatriate' scholar who is obliged to remain in Paris till the completion of his doctoral dissertation. He falls in love with the French woman Madeleine who is five years older in age. Being a college lecturer she has an income which proves of substantial help to the couple. His marriage with Madeleine gives him indeed an economic advantage. But some of Raja Rao's critics have pointed out that it is because of this advantage that Rama is attracted to her. This is a cynical interpretation of a romantic affair. His sincerity to her is never doubted until their final moment together. As things subsequently turn out one wonders whether Rama had not had an inkling or an accompanying awareness of the consequences that would follow upon his marrying outside his Indian society which meant ostracizing himself from his family's cultural tradition. He might have realized that his decision entailed a heavy sacrifice. He would be disturbing the whole family by inducting into it an alien of a different culture who would neither grasp the age-old ethos of the Hindu tradition nor be able to communicate with anyone notwithstanding the fact that the family desires to give her all the affection that she deserves as daughter-in-law. One can recall the moment when Rama's Little Mother carries the photograph of Madeleine and her child into the sanctuary of her gods and sprinkles flowers upon it to bless them and pray for their life and prosperity.

However, the first flush of Rama's dream of a romantic union with the French lady does not last long and the marriage begins to flounder leading to their final estrangement. A communication gap between them has been gradually developing. As C.D. Narasimhaiah has noted, it is a moot point in the novel to say what exactly is the cause of their estrangement.[5] Yet, I believe, that the author seems to have thrown in some hints which beckon to the cause.

The breach of faith occurs on two specific occasions. When Madeleine loses her son Rama is not there to console her. Consequently, she has to bear the shock of the calamity alone. No doubt, he had been away in India to perform the last rites of his deceased father, visiting holy places such as Benares, Allahabad, etc. But when he returns to France and learns of the tragic death of his own son the expression of his grief is inadequate and even superficial. His seeming unconcern is sufficient to shock Madeleine into a state of revolution. Her disinterestedness in him paves the way for her intellectual involvement and absorption in spiritual life through a determined rejection of marriage and renunciation of the family ties with Rama. Buddhism being for her an already familiar and cultivated area she readily turns to it both for solace and for a substitute to fill in the void. She is convinced that it alone could show her a way out of her *vairagya* (extremity of despair). Having experienced the tragic reality of life first hand on her pulses she is awakened into a new life. She sets out on the very path of renunciation once traversed by the Prince of Kapilvastu and abandons her spiritually unawakened husband. This is how she chooses to resolve the crisis facing her. She might have acted somewhat differently had she not turned to Buddhism. Had she retained her Catholic faith she might have turned to a nunnery or become a VAD like Celia Coplestone in *The Cocktail Party* when faced with a crisis situation in her personal life.[6]

Madeleine's awareness of Rama's fascination for Savithri when the latter stays with them for a week in Paris may be underlined as another important factor in the widening of their communication gap. This must have given Madeleine more reason to pursue her intellectual goal with greater earnestness and get lost in Buddhistic studies. Likewise, Rama's ritual marriage with Savithri in London strongly inclines him toward realizing that the ultimate purpose of his intellectual pursuit in Paris is different: he will not write a dissertation or gather experience as an 'expatriate' scholar but acquire knowledge of the self and the cultural tradition he belongs to. His marriage being on the rocks, his yearning for strengthening the cultural bond with his home country drives him to reflect more deeply than before on the philosophical dimensions of Indian cultural tradition of which he already possesses considerable awareness and grasp. In his research also he had undertaken to link up and trace similarities and parallels between the origin and history of the Cathars and the origin and history of his Vedic ancestors, the Abigensenians. Rama's research deepens his interest in Indian cultural tradition. But his absorption in his metaphysical pursuit further distances him from Madeleine and widens the breach between them.

There is yet another possible reason for the widening communication gap between the couple. It relates to their intellectual differences on the implication of the word 'Hindutav' or the Hinduness of a Hindu emphasized by Hinduism. Madeleine is bewildered on becoming aware that she could not become a true Brahmin wife she had chosen to become despite her flawless sincerity and loyalty to her Hindu husband evident from her service to and concern for him when he is ailing. Could anyone in her position feel happy to know that the Hindu religious precepts and dogmas allowed her only a lower status in society than that accorded to any Indian woman just because she was not essentially a Brahmin by birth? She must have painfully realized that she would be recognized as a true Brahmin only after she was cremated according to Vedic (Hindu) rituals. Considering the boldness with which this situation is presented in the novel it appears that Raja Rao underlines the evil of the discouraging and limiting factor in the Indian cultural tradition and tempers it with his emphasis on the spirit of freedom in love and marriage. It is in that spirit that the affair between the two foreigners is developed into a marital relationship. It is another matter that the parties concerned fail to respect their marital bond and break off. Breakdown in marriages is a commonplace phenomenon in the west. But Raja Rao surely takes pains to bring into ridicule the stringent orthodoxy of the Brahminical culture and desires to emphasize the human aspect of such relationships. This is manifest from the orthodox Hindu Rama's falling in love with the orthodox Catholic Madeleine in Paris and trying to emotionally understand her religious faith and ritual for he believes that 'to win your love means to win her gods.' Similarly, by marrying him Madeleine puts Christianity behind her, and embraces his Hinduism. Critics accuse her of being false to her Christian faith and of being tempted to become a Brahmin wife. While each tries to understand the other's faith and culture it is Rama the expatriate scholar who by his nostalgic reminiscences seems to be inclined to put greater weight on the desirability of understanding his own culture. He recognizes in Savithri the sort of ideal Indian woman that he missed out in Madeleine despite her nobility and selflessness. That is precisely one more reason for the communication gap becoming unbridgeable and for Madeleine to ask for divorce. One might note that the scene in the novel in which Maitre Sigon repeatedly asks about who had proposed the divorce first unambiguously underlines Rama's responsibility for the breach, not Madeleine's. A recent critic Shyamala Narayan[7] follows Raja Rao himself and other critics in support of the view that Madeleine is responsible for the marriage breakdown. But there is also a host of critics who support the contrary view. D.S. Maini holds Ramaswamy guilty for his "metaphysic of promiscuity."[8] Esha Dey finds him guilty of "compulsive self-deception"[9] while Vimala Rao credits Madeleine for her "respect for the institution of marriage . . . [and for being] more of an Indian than the Westernized Savithri."[10] It would perhaps be appropriate to blame the breakdown of Rama-Madeleine marriage as much on Rama himself as on the narrow-mindedness of the Hindu cultural tradition which tabooed his marriage with a Western girl, by denying her full social recognition. I am quite in agreement with Paul Sharrad (92) when he differs with Raja Rao himself, who puts the blame on Madeleine, on the ground that the text itself contradicts its author. The text surely points to the moral failure and guilt of Ramaswamy.

It is only natural that as soon as Rama's artificial link with France through Madeleine is snapped that the confused, dilemma-ridden protagonist suddenly realizes the loss of his home in Paris and decides to embark for Travancore in quest of his spiritual Guru. But his failure in marriage and the thought of having betrayed Madeleine leave behind in his mind a sense of guilt which although he expresses no regrets at what has happened yet he experiences further alienation from life. He believes that on his return to India he might restore his loosened links with his family culture but he cannot free himself of the sense of guilt. On the contrary, Madeleine suffers several shocks which give her greater determination to pursue her spiritual insight. Her announcement of divorce catches Rama (as well as the reader) unawares and gives him a shock of surprise. It seals off their estrangement. The shock is intense because she tells Rama to marry an Indian woman near his age which undoubtedly hints at her awareness of his covert desire for and relationship with Savithri. One can understand that she is hurt because she perceives in Rama a greater desire for carnal rather than spiritual companionship that the marriage was meant to be. Perhaps Savithri might have been a desirable alternative from various angles but he was already married. It is rather mystifying that even when she desperately sends for him to rescue her from Pratap just before her marriage Rama fails to respond to her call. He might have been feeling guilty of failure on her account too, particularly because of the ritualistic marriage with her he had performed in London while Madeleine was in Paris. Instead of rushing out to her rescue he spends that fateful night of Savithri's marriage with Laxmi in Bombay. His forbidding moral looseness cannot be condoned even though it indicates as one critic describes it, "a comic presaging of the matrimonial disorder in his own life."[11] In short all these acts of Rama must leave some imprints on his mind. No wonder then that he is in a dilemma and therefore decides one dreadful night to begin his journey of expiation by travelling to Travancore in quest of his *guru* (the intercessor) precisely in the manner in which the Chamberlaynes in *The Cocktail Party* who are threatened with a similar marital breakdown decide to go to the psychiatrist 'guru' who shows them the ways to salvation.

The setting off of the estranged couple on their journeys not in the western but in the Indian style of expiation in two ways—the renunciation in the Vedic/Upanishadic way adopted by Rama—gives the narrative an unexpected turn at the end which is discomfitting. While the novel borders on the verge of a tragedy, it ends on a spiritual note which comes as an anti-climax to the main narrative. The ending leaves several issues unresolved—the cause of failure of love-marriage, the precise nature of the transcendental experiences and the unexplored sense of guilt in the protagonist. The ending of the novel may be a logical consequence of the despair and shaken confidence of Rama at the humiliating conclusion of his relationship with Madeleine. But this ending does not strengthen but weakens the author's chance of developing the fine tragic potential of the novel and converts it into a melodrama.

The attempted meeting between the East and the West through the conjugal union of Rama and Madeleine ends in a failure. The East-West encounter culminates in an unresolvable cocktail. The two different cultural streams have not coalesced even at individual personal levels. While Rama returns, though less firmly, to his cultural tradition, Madeleine instead of returning to the Catholic faith embraces Buddhism with greater conviction and determination. The couple thus separate and work out their own salvations along the two divergent paths shown by Hinduism and Buddhism.

But it would be wrong to think that the East-West encounter has totally failed. Rama surely gets one important benefit from his encounter with the French culture represented by Madeleine. He gets an opportunity to peep into his own self. The desire for self-knowledge is born in him via his experience as an 'expatriate' in the west.

His inquisitive and intellectual wandering in Eastern and Western religions and philosophical traditions and locales awaken in him a desire for self-knowledge. This indirectly helps him to rediscover his past and get over an inner feeling of being an 'orphan': "I was born an orphan, and have remained one. I have wandered the world and have sobbed in hotel rooms and in trains, have looked at the cold mountains and sobbed, for I had no mother. One day and that was when I was twenty-two, I sat in an hotel—it was in the Pyrenese—and I sobbed, for I knew I would never see my mother again." (7)

The significance of Rama's sense of isolation and feeling like an orphan can be better understood in the Indian religious context. Every Indian Hindu sees himself if not directly as an orphan but surely as a child-like figure craving for the blessings of the mother—the concept of mother extends to include the consciousness of the mother as goddess.

This is evident from Rama's feeling of eternal isolation from the mother when he reminisces the childhood scene of her death: "When she died they covered her with white flowers . . . they took her to the burning ghat. They shaved me completely, and when they returned they gave me bengal-gram and some sweets. I could not understand what had happened. Nor do I understand it now. I know my mother, my mother Gauri, is not dead, and yet I am an orphan. Am I always going to be an orphan?"

The sense of his being eternally an orphan despite the mother Gauri watching over him is suggestive of a deep craving for the blessings of the mother-goddess Gauri, wife of Lord Shiva, the preserver and destroyer of life in the Hindu mythology. The feeling of being eternally an orphan is the Indian equivalent of the western man's sense of loneliness and alienation. As C.D. Narasimhaiah has pointed out, the feeling of the loneliness of human situation deeprooted in the West's concept of life is felt differently in the Indian view of life. In the West this view of the essential human situation is conveyed through "preoccupation with a sick conscience as in the novels, in different degrees, of Camus, Moravia, Greene and Silone,"[13] or as in the works of T.S. Eliot. Those novels are filled with "a rancour that is contemptuous of immortality and will not let us recognize what is divine in us." (84-85) In *The Serpent and the Rope* Raja Rao makes an admirable attempt to focus on this deeprooted craving of a sensitive mind for *moksha*—that is, freedom from the cycle of life, death and rebirth—through the experience of seeing God face to face without disturbing the artistic form of the narrative. Rama is a sensitive protagonist with a craving for self-knowledge but this craving is obstructed by the feeling of sin-guilt which is not distinctly focused upon. Consequently, his image as a sensitive protagonist is somewhat blurred. The sense of guilt is felt within but it does not persecute him as it might have persecuted a protagonist of a western sensibility. It is here that one begins to feel that in his protagonist Raja Rao attempts to blend Indian and Western sensibilities but their fusion is difficult to achieve because the two sensibilities represent two fundamentally different ways of fulfilling that craving for salvation. One follows the Negative way of Renunciation of life and the world; the other follows the Positive Way of Affirmation of life as well as the Negative Way of Renunciation. Both the ways are illustrated by T.S. Eliot's *The Cocktail Party* to which *The Serpent and the Rope* bears an interesting parallel. In *The Serpent and the Rope* both Rama as well as Madeleine pursue the Negative Way of Renunciation but in slightly different ways. While Madeleine directly announces her renunciation of marriage by divorce and commitment to Buddhistic study, Rama has a sudden realization that he must journey back to India in quest of a spiritual guru who can with the traces of the ancient sage Yagnyawalkya in him help his disciple to work out his salvation.

That Raja Rao makes a commendable effort to bring into harmony the Western and Eastern sensibilities and perceptions can be seen in the delightful description of the coronation of Queen Elizabeth in which Rama too participates, or in the presentation of a close view of life and culture of France and England and India. The embittered atmosphere of India's pre-Independence relations with Britain is superceded by a cheerful atmosphere of friendship and equality which suffuses their relations in the post-Independence era. (Raja Rao retrospectively looks back from 1960, the year of publication of *The Serpent and the Rope,* to the year 1947 when India obtained freedom from the British rule.) To say that Raja Rao's emphasis in the novel is entirely on the exposition of Hindu cultural tradition in the light of the Sanskritic philosophical ideas is to deny the artistic merit of the novel. Accordingly, the view held by some critics that *The Serpent and the Rope* is a philosophical or metaphysical novel when it does not undertake to give any systematic exposition of any philosophical system does not carry much conviction. As Shyamala Narayan has pointed out,[12] Rao's protagonist makes several errors in the exposition of some of the philosophical concepts discussed by him which puts a question mark on the form of the novel.

However, it may be possible to argue that *The Serpent and the Rope* is a metaphysical comedy of the same pattern as T.S. Eliot's *The Cocktail Party.* Like the protagonists in Eliot's play, the protagonists of Rao's novel are concerned with the exercise of their choices which instead of establishing them in their different social settings lead them toward different transcendental experiences and goals. The progression of their perceptions from the personal to social to transcendental planes is achieved through the ironic mode of comedy which makes these protagonists the unaware agents of a divine design. Since the novel devotes a major portion of its length to the portrayal of its Indian protagonist Ramaswamy, it can safely be said that the novel is an ironical representation of a modern Indian intellectual who despite his immensity and range of knowledge of Western and Eastern cultural traditions reveals his inadequacy of grasp of the very fundamentals of the glorious, age-old metphysical tradition of his own country. Rama travels to France and England to pursue his research and, in the process, educates himself about the life and history of Europe. But for the knowledge of his cultural tradition he depends mainly on memory of what he had learnt and experienced in India in his childhood. The implication is that he ought to be firmly committed to his own cultural tradition as well. The research into the identity of the Cathars and the Abigensenians indirectly leads him into a quest for his own identity. The quest for identity becomes an important theme of the novel, but this theme is also significant for its implication that the protagonist needs greater scholarly commitment to the understanding of his own culture. The journey to the west is therefore an eye-opener and necessitates a journey back to India. But until he really achieves that self-knowledge it would be equally valid to maintain that it is not Ramaswamy but Madeleine who is at the centre of the narrative deserving our acclaim for her suffering and her commitment to the new faith that she has chosen. Compared to her, Rama looks like a loose, immoral prig who only raves about high-strung Indian philosophical concepts, who achieves practically little and rather shifts loosely from Madeleine to Savithri to Laxmi to sublimate his carnal desires. One can only hope that his restless and intrepid spirit is harnessed into a meaningful transcendental pursuit under the direction of the spiritual guru at Travancore. To attain that spiritual vision he may need a dip in the Ganges and a spell of meditation on the Himalayas. A caution is sounded because there might be redherrings to obstruct and mislead him on the way. Comically, the attention is drawn to the Brahmins of Benares who fleece the visitor to the holy city. They impel him to perform various rituals to obtain the blessings of the gods who are held by them in their custody. Ironically, these pseudo-Brahmins are the preservers of India's cultural tradition. Rama is a modern intellectual who has yet to be a true 'Brahmin,' a definition of which is given at the opening page of *The Serpent and the Rope*—'Brahmin is he who knows Brahman.' The implication is that today's Brahmin is in a state of degradation because he seeks not God but alms and material welfare. C.D. Narasimhaiah has aptly connected "the vulgar politician and the present-day intellectual, a descendant of the decadent Brahmin," (78) are alike in that they have brought the cultural tradition into utter shame and degradation by their commercial interests and neglect of the cultural heritage.

To conclude, then, we may concede that in *The Serpent and the Rope* Rao not only recaptures the cultural tradition of India vis-a-vis the European cultural tradition and writes an interesting novel on the subject. He also uses the ironical mode of representation to achieve his object. He castigates the present-day Indian intellectual for sidetracking the rich cultural heritage of India which offers the Indian vision of the way to self-knowledge and salvation. The Indian protagonist of the novel wanders in the west in search of a knowledge (is Raja Rao self-critical too for his wandering in the west?) which is of minor academic significance because, like Madam Sosostris in Eliot's *The Waste Land* (to which several critics have referred for comparison with certain elements in the novel) he has lost the spiritual vision. He had, like the ancient Indian hermit, better wander back to the Ganges and up the Himalayas or into the Vedas and the Upanishads and Sankara's philosophy to recover the lost vision. It would be quite in place to say that working as they are toward the same goal—that is, writing their metaphysical comedies, one in the drama and the other in the novel form—both T.S. Eliot and Raja Rao make the modern intellectual-quester protagonist look back to the Himalayas and the Ganges for the possibility of spiritual regeneration of man.

NOTES

1. (London: John Murray, 1960).
2. *Raja Rao and Cultural Tradition* (New Delhi: 1987), p. 91.
3. The desire for male offspring was regarded essential to preservation of the family line and was therefore central to patriarchal religion and the early institutions of the principle races of Europe and Asia, in Greece, Rome, and India. See Samuel Johnson, *Indian and Oriental Religions* (New Delhi, 1983), pp. 205-6.
4. Jawaharlal Nehru, in his *Discovery of India*, has succinctly dealt with the Indian view of life and pointed out that "Both principles [life-negation and life-affirmation] are present in varying degrees in all the old religions and cultures. But I should have thought that Indian culture, taken as a whole, never emphasized the negation of life, though some of its philosophies did so?" (Calcutta, 1946), p. 82.
5. *Raja Rao* (Arnold-Heinemann), p. 105.
6. I do not agree with the view that "she would have saved her marriage" had she stuck to her Catholic faith. See K.R. Rao, "Raja Rao and the Metaphysical Novel," in G.S. Amur et al, ed., *Indian Readings in Commonwealth Literature* (New Delhi: Sterling, 1985), p. 90.
7. *Raja Rao: Man and His Works,* p. 66.
8. "Raja Rao's Vision, Values and Aesthetic" in *Perspectives on Raja Rao*, ed. K.K. Sharma, p. 9. Cf. Shyamala Narayan, p. 61.
9. "Fissures in Being: Anguish and Alienation in *The Serpent and the Rope,*" Cf. Shyamala Narayan, p. 60.

10. Cf. Shyamala Narayan, p. 60.
11. K.R. Rao, p. 89.
12. See Shyamala Narayan, *Raja Rao: Man and His Works*, pp. 50-51. She has also dealt with this aspect of the novel in her article, "Ramaswamy's Erudition: A Note on Raja Rao's *The Serpent and the Rope*," *Ariel* (October 1983), Vol. XIV, No. 4, pp. 6-17.

In Quest of Form: A Study of Structural Motifs in Salman Rushdie's *Midnight's Children*

SEEMA BHADURI

The great diversity of themes, narrative techniques and stylistic devices that have gone into the making of *Midnight's Children*,[1] and the intricacy of its formal arrangement, seem to defy any attempt at a comprehensive analysis of its structural pattern. This paper however, attempts to draw out certain basic structural motifs and patterns of narrative design underlying the novel's close approximation to the variegated collective life of the Indian subcontinent during the turbulent period of its modern history.

A historical survey of English fiction would show that the temporal configuration of the novel has changed from time to time in keeping with changes in the age's/writer's perception of the nature of time and reality. The imaginative architectonics of the nineteenth century English fiction was shaped by the logistics of rationalism which focused on the causal patterns of social relationships. The temporal organization of the narratives along such a pattern was exclusively linear. In modernist fiction, the novelist sought to capture the dynamics of the very process of the individual's experience as she/he stood alone among the debris of a crumbling faith, faced with new, sometimes horrifying insights into her/his own self and the external world—the alien medium in which to be. This switchover to an entirely subjective interpretation of life legitimized patterns of experience, and consequently, modes of narration hitherto uncommon. The Existentialists placing the individual against an alien and unpredictable world, focused on the problem of his confrontation with it in a primal experiential state where time and space were not mere objective referents, but conflicting determinals where the internal and the external worlds met as strangers. In the narrative exposition of this experience, dream and fantasy, the surreal and the absurd, all flocked into the pages of the novel, dramatizing the mindscape or the conflict, moulding and remoulding time. But modernist fiction was still an extreme form of psychological realism framed around the still collectively recognized entities of society, character and values, though the one was crumbling down; the second related now to personal impressions and conflicts of self and identity rather than to matters of conduct and decorum, and the third concerned, again, matters of self rather than of social ethics.

Post-modernist fiction on the other hand, is primarily concerned with two things—the portrayal of the late-capitalist Western society which, spinning the whirl of technology wrought change and in the absence of the stable base of society and character, appears an ahistorical, temporal fantasy to the writer's now necessarily subjective eye, rendering fantasy the most common idiom of narrative expression, and in keeping with this view of reality, the demonstration of the fictive nature of the text itself.[2] This brought about another transformation in the temporal alignment of the narrative. Fantasy and documentary realism overlap here to show the seamless convergence of fact and fancy, the one substantiating the other in an elastic spatio-temporal medium.

In *Midnight's Children* Rushdie uses post-modernist techniques to create a sort of 'magic realism' that offers a comprehensive vision of the multi-dimensional Indian reality. The novel is held together by a pattern of interlaced motifs. The controlling structural motif in the narrative is the Saleem-Padma relationship. Padma is no ordinary mistress and listener. Less and more than a character, she is the narrator's counterself, the 'other' in the mind's "intrinsic dualism and duplicity" which makes a person's "inmost profoundest being essentially dramatic."[3] She enables Rushdie to translate "all [Saleem's] thinking in terms of process"—to dramatize it.[4] Through her 'paradoxical earthiness of spirit' her 'ignorance and superstition' led demands for linear narratives, she serves as 'counterweight to [Saleem's] miracle-laden omniscience' (150) and 'keeps[his] feet on the ground,' ensuring thereby the progression and formal integrity of the narrative, so much so that Saleem credits her with mothering the narrative. By likening Saleem and Padma to the creator Brahma and to Laxmi, Rushdie employs the Hindu myth of cosmic creation to explain the very process of creation (here, Saleem's creation of a fictive universe) and its relation thereby, to Time. According to this myth, the Universe is 'Maya'—an illusory dream of the Lord wherein reality is what it is believed to be. (211)

In *Midnight's Children* 'Maya' becomes a metaphor—for the illusory nature of reality portrayed by Rushdie. Brahma's dream however becomes a reality only when it is offered a spatio-temporal existence by Laxmi whose second name is Padma. Saleem's Padma thus becomes 'Mother of Time.' (194)

Brahma's dream, in case of Saleem, becomes wild flights of imagination, of visions, and recollections—atemporal fancies. But Padma, preoccupied with the earthly—temporal phenomena of marriage and birth, forces Saleem down from time to time to the narration of actual events, i.e. into linear progression the one characteristic essential to any existence in time i.e. in reality. Rushdie is here grounding his 'magic-realism'—his use of myth, memory and fantasy, in the larger context of the Indian view of reality. Moreover, he gives them precedence over temporal reality. Time begins with birth, but birth is from seed, which, in case of creative arts, is imagination. This happens to be 'above present and past,' and writer Saleem's forte. (194) One finds therefore that the narrative moves back from event and birth to their inception in mind and thought. The narrative begins, for instance, with Saleem's birth, but, in order to account for it, Saleem travels 32 years back to the point where his grandfather lost his faith and was thereby led into marrying Naseem Banu who espoused their family. Similarly, the blood-drops on the perforated sheet, marking the beginnings of Aziz's history, are preceded by the 3 blood-drops from Aziz's nose—signs of his loss of faith, the ideational ground for his history. The allusion to the Quranic myth of Creation, again precedes this latter even as the source of Rushdie's own idea.

Padma is also called the "lotus-goddess of the present." (150) The present as the moment of being and becoming, of transfiguration, becomes evident from another appellate of Padma's—Saleem calls her the "dung-lotus." (102) The emphasis falls equally on 'dung' (base material/earth), the hyphen (transformational phase) and lotus (aesthetic incarnation or form), because hyphens play an important role in Saleem's cosmos. They serve as 'modes of connections' in 'dualistically combined configurations of opposites' that constitute reality. Reality for Saleem would therefore mean a perpetual state of transfiguration i.e. impermanence (238) as will be explained later.

As an ordinary listener, an ignorance and superstition-ridden woman who is interested only in 'what-comes-next,' Padma represents the masses with their no-nonsense-footing in down-to-earth reality. A piece of literature must conform to the laws of this reality, draw the belief of the listeners, then transcend it for the purpose of its imaginative and aesthetic integrity. Through his reported dialogues with Padma, wherein he assures us he has satisfied her demands for literality, Saleem does precisely this and sets himself free for his 'fancy-talk.'

Padma serves yet another technical function by being witness to the narrator's corporeal self, for his persona is otherwise too 'grotesque' (109) for conviction. Almost every chapter in the novel contains both the (reported) Saleem Padma dialogue on the present state of his health or narrative, and Saleem's past experiences. This makes for the effect of simultaneity. Without Padma Saleem would have had to be 'reconciled to the narrow one-dimensionality of a straight line,' that cannot project a multi-dimensional reality.

Padma and Saleem together make the feminine-masculine polarity of a single self as well as the Hindu-Muslim combine of the Indian cultural plurality. In this first they represent what Rushdie expounds throughout the novel—the essentially dual nature of all reality. In the second they personify the multiplicity of the Indian culture—again a major theme of *Midnight's Children*.

The theme of the dual nature of all reality is condensed in the Saleem-Shiva motif. The two form the split halves of a single-self, joined together by a prophesy (87) and the moment of their birth. They embody the split in the educated Indian's orientation to life, wrought by the Western influence. Narrator Saleem is haunted on the one hand by the ancient oriental world-view personified in Tai and projected in the mountains and skies of Kashmir, and on the other, by the clock-ridden world of 'things, things, things' personified in Shiva. Tai's view of an ageless organic cosmos was forfeited by his protege Aadam Aziz—Saleem's grandfather—whose western education robbed him of his faith, replacing it with a dubious belief in history and material science. He could neither believe nor disbelieve in God. This 'fractured' vision is inherited by Saleem. (275) But Tai's influence on Aziz's personality is strong. His nose, the blue of his eyes and his laughter all echo Tai's ways, and the picture, hanging on the wall of Saleem's bed-room, of the old boatman pointing his finger to the Western horizon where the sun is sinking while a young European is listening to him—all speak of Tai's invisible presence in Saleem's life and thoughts. The picture, a prophetic image of the future, grows in significance upon the growing Saleem.

But even the rest of the affluent inhabitants of Methwold Estate with their English life style, cannot do without sadhus, soothsayers, ghosts and godmen. The split is evident in them too. Only Shiva has been sold out to western values and in him Saleem finds a formidable opponent to his value-based ideas (304) he inherited from his grandfather.

This dichotomy of vision becomes part of the larger dichotomy plaguing the historical world-view ushered in by Aziz. In trying to sift truth from untruth while reconstructing his experiences, narrator Saleem finds that reality is assailed by "the unchanging twoness of things." A beginning is also an end. "Alpha is Omega too." (141) He says, "Shiva and Saleem, Victor and Victim, understand our rivalry and you will gain an understanding of the age in which you live." (432) Even historical events, when viewed from the underside, lose their uni-dimensional veracity. For instance, Saleem discovers that the Emergency has two parts—white and black. (421) 'Objectivity' becomes a myth when the "quasi-osmotic interpenetration of things"[5] and the intervention of chance or 'ambiguity' in natural processes (141) are taken into account. In order therefore to expose the fluid nature of reality Rushdie yokes together paradoxes and contrasting perspectives so that any given situation becomes at once serious and trivial, sublime and gross, ordinary and bizarre. Each cancels the other out, dissolving the certitude accompanying 'objective reality,' into one might say, a sort of nothing-ness, supporting if indirectly Tai's view of an ageless, changeless cosmic order.

In order to project the collective experience of the Indian reality Rushdie employs four time-lines in the novel. The cosmic scale, ageless and unchanging and personified in Tai, becomes the continuous back-drop against which the historical time must run its course. It is not a passive back-drop, however, for Rushdie alludes to the Maha-Yuga cycles of the Brahmanic cosmology (Tai's world-view) to laugh the date/clock obsessed historical time-line which "began on Friday, February 18th, 3102 B.C. and will last a mere 432000 years!" into perspective. (194) Besides, it remained the ultimate desired destination for Saleem. Tai, the voice of the eternal mountains of Kashmir, symbolized a world of timeless cosmic harmony. Saleem, living in the world of materialism and clock time i.e. of 'Shiva and the Angel' (of Death) would 'die with Kashmir on his lips.' (462-63)

The second time-line projects the collective unconscious of the Indian masses. Here the past is held secure in mythic memories while the new political myths of the historical present, such as democracy and votes for women, are seen to have made little impact. (245) This collective consciousness is very much at home among the trappings of modern technology, and ghosts and God exist comfortably at Methwold Estate along with Narlikar's tetrapods that reclaimed land from sea.[6] (176)

The third time-line is that of history. Historical time began when the English 'discovered' India bringing with them the clock and the calender. In the novel, Aadam Aziz, German-returned and expelled from Kashmir by Tai, became, on having lost faith, vulnerable to "women and history," (10) married for money and joined the Indian struggle against the British. Tai, significantly, had wanted the Kashmir valley which was protected naturally by its mountains, to remain free of all political/historical/temporal affiliations. He died in 1948 while fighting all alone against the Indian and Pakistani armies marching into it.

Rushdie treats of history from the 'underside,' exposing the differential impact of events on different sections of the population. This treatment is in line with Fernand Brandel's 'longue duree' view of history[7] which argues that rather than concentrate on 'the most capricious and delusive' 'short-time span' which deals only with major events and front-line actors, historical study should move from surface to the depth, from event to structure and model back to the event. In *Midnight's Children* India's hour of independance, for instance, is projected by snippets of Nehru's speech in the Parliament interspersed with Amina's labour pains, street celebrations, ravaging fires, police hunts and desperate railway-station crowds. Such montage, representing the writer's multiple vision, 'dislodges history from chronometric time'[8] to expose the often contradictory realities hidden underneath its official unilinear versions. (115-16) Rushdie further believes that personal experience is the only authentic version of history. So memory becomes the only representative of truth. (211) Therefore the mercuro-chrome stains on Aadam Aziz must represent Indian blood spilled by the British, and the compulsory sterilization of the Midnight's children must certify the repressive nature of the Emergency.

The fourth time-line pertains to the individual's (i.e. Saleem's) consciousness which includes everything within it, (383) along with the durational structures of his own personal experiences. This is the main narrative time-line. Saleem's consciousness becomes both the field of exploration and the source of projection, both the manifestation and the orchestrator of this multitudinous reality. The orchestration of reality is effected by strings of consciousness—memory and imagination, which detect and aesthetically develop the form hidden within this multiverse of time-lines and things.

There is on every page of the narrative, a sort of cosmic fluidity in which things, events, characters, places, collide with one another. Only the narrator's memory and imagination, like some deft potter's hand, turns out an art form from this multiverse of ceaseless activity. (240)

Consciousness becomes a motif that serves like the Brahma-Laxmi myth/motif to impart a fluid, elastic texture to the narrative so that Rushdie's experiments with truth find their basis in the truth of the psychological nature of the consciousness. In many ways, it also structures the temporal framework of the narrative. As consciousness in itself is always of the present, embodying both past and the idea of futurity, so in the narrative of *Midnight's Children* past and present are simultaneous: "whatever you were is forever who you are" (368) says Saleem. His two selves—protagonist and narrator—exist simultaneously in the narrative, with every chapter dwelling on both the narratorial present and the autobiographical past. He finds that they are both different and similar. (167) The simultaneity of the past-carried-in-memory with the present appears in the narrative through summary repetition of past events at intervals and through the use of the present tense to narrate past events. (106-7) 'Memory's ways' also account for the breaks in temporal sequence and lateral incursions of divergent topics. There are also the leaps in time or 'previews' as Uma Parameswaran calls them,[9] involving the anticipatory mention of events and persons coming up much later in the narrative. These belong to the oral traditions of story-telling which Rushdie adapts in his novels. They are part of Rushdie's technique of first-person narration, and where he is present before the reader as the narrator protagonist who 'knows it-all.'

The narrative, with all its fantastic complexities, is held together by Saleem's search for form (meaning) in his life. As narrator he realizes that his life as protagonist consists "an excess of intertwined lives, events, miracles, places, rumours" (9) from which, with the aid of memory, imagination and art he will have to recreate the form of his life.

Saleem's quest for form is expressed through the motif of a journey in which Aadam Aziz and he are involved in expanding tiers. Within the pages of the narrative Aziz travels from Kashmir to Amritsar to Agra to Bombay, then back to Agra and finally to Kashmir. His journey is circular. Saleem's journey takes him on an even enlarging spiral pattern thus: from Bombay to Delhi and back; then from Bombay to Karachi and back; next from Bombay to Karachi to Dhaka to Benares to Delhi and finally back to Bombay. The two journeys are symbolic.[10] To both Aziz and Saleem, Tai's Kashmir stands for completeness/perfection. Aziz had to leave Kashmir on losing his faith in Tai's world-view. His return to belief in God is deceptive. (276, 80) Furthermore, he did not regain his lost faith—he 'hated' God.

Therefore, though Aziz returns to Kashmir, he is unable to climb up the hill which overlooks the valley that had been his home. These journeys are thus journeys of experience and symbolic of an awakening consciousness. Aziz failed, until the end, to diagnose the cause of his failure in life. Narrator Saleem on the other hand, acquires by means of these journeys, the understanding and the vision that enables him to put the history of his life into perspective. He writes: "condemned by a perforated sheet to a life of fragments . . . I have nevertheless done better than my grandfather; because while Aadam Aziz remained the sheet's victim, I have become its master—and Padma is the one who is now under its spell." (121)

The perforated sheet replicates the metaphorical 'hole' that developed in Aziz's heart when he lost faith (12) making him victim to women and history. The landowner Ghani traps Aziz into marriage with his daughter by means of this sheet. Saleem, born to Aziz's daughter Amina also inherits his grandfather's 'fragmented' vision.

While the circular route of Aziz's journey signifies a sort of completion i.e. death, the spiral route, lacking an innate terminating point, leads Saleem's evolving consciousness not to death, but to 'release' into the general life-stream. (463)

Saleem's quest for meaning is expressed variously as the quest for identity and the search for a father. The former leads him by way of a search for 'purpose' in life, to the ambitious project of defending the country. (152-54) This draws him into the vortex of history and unmans him, so that, he finally arrives at the conclusion that "the small, individual lives of men" are preferable to "macrocosmic' ambitions." (435) The latter quest is metaphorical.

Saleem was brought into the world by Anita and William Methwold—the mother died at childbirth and the father left before he was born. This fact remained unknown, however, until he had outgrown his childhood, while his father's identity remained unknown to all but him. It was generally believed that Anita had her child from one circus clown-singer called We Willie Winki (we will wink?) (102)

Saleem's eyes and nose however resembled those of Aadam Aziz in whose home he was bred, as son to Aziz's daughter Amina.

While the result of this double (multiple?), mutually contradictory parentage becomes evident in the contradiction between Saleem's world (physical Methwold begotten) and vision (Aziz begotten), it also leads him into the search for a genuine father, and he acquires many by the way. This situation can be viewed in the overall context of the treatment of the father-figure in Western post-modernist fiction. Patricia Dreschel Tobin traces the origin of the revolt against the idea of linear time in Western fiction to the rejection of the patrilinear pattern of the family wherein all persons/events derived from/were links in a single chain of causality that had begun at some point with a father-figure.

Tobin refers to Sterne as the predecessor of the post-modernist line of thinking, who had dismissed "consciousness and structure as a muddle" and had called causality an extraneous imposition of the mind which "working contrary to the randomness of experiences . . . reduces possibilities, covers man with meaning and ignores any cosmos beyond society's norms."[11]

In *Midnight's Children* too Rushdie debunks the idea of linearity/patrilinearity—the line of causation becomes multi-lateral with too many fathers having been "pressed into service in the absence of

William Methwold." (436) Yet Saleem does perceive a line of descent—howsoever discontinuous in terms of chronometric time, from Tai, via Aziz, to himself and then onto his son Aadam Sinai, for, even this last one had blue eyes "the blue of recurrence, the fateful blue of Kashmir sky." Besides, he was the true great grandson of Aziz, as well as the 'synthesis' of Saleem and Shiva. (420-25) Recurrence—repetition of the past—becomes a major feature of Rushdie's treatment of history.

So structure and causality, do exist, asserts Saleem: "Everything has shape, if you look for it. There is no escape from form." (226) This form is the meaning (461) which lies not in "variable and . . . inconstant" time (106) which is the field of the equally variable and inconstant reality, but in the 'truth' beyond it. (79)

NOTES

1. Salman Rushdie, *Midnight's Children* (London: Picador, 1982).
2. Malcolm Bradbury, *The Novel Today* (Glasgow: Fontana, 1982), p. 15.
3. Friedrich Schlegal, "The Ironic Consciousness," *The Modern Tradition*, ed. Richard Ellman and Charles Feidelson (New York: Oxford University Press, 1965), p. 738.
4. Soren Kierkegaard, "Indirect Communication," *The Modern Tradition*, p. 744.
5. Klaus Borner, "The Reception of *Midnight's Children* in W. Germany," *The Commonwealth Review*, I, 2, p. 119.
6. This method of treating time has also been employed by Garcia Marquez *in One Hundred Years of Solitude* The people of both India and Latin America share a common view of time rejecting the notion of historical progression in which the past is irretrievably lost. According to Jaime Mejia Dugue "because Latin America has preserved in its social structures whole epochs which in the Western world passed by in successive order. Latin American man knows only the reality of simultaneity, never the reality of succession and continuity." "Nito Realidad en Gabriel Garcia Marquez," *Bogota Editorial La Oveja Negra* (1970), p. 28, 41-49 in Patricia Dreschel Tobin, *Time and the Novel: The Geneological Imperative* (Princeton: Princeton University Press, 1978), p. 169.
7. Maurice Aymard and Harbans Mukhia, ed. *French Studies in History,* vol. I, *The Inheritance* (Delhi: Orient Longman, 1988), p. 335.

8. Uma Parameswaran, "Handcuffed to History: Salman Rushdie's Art," *Ariel*, vol. 14, no. 4 (Oct. 1983), p. 38.
9. *Ibid.* Also refer to Tobin, p. 182 for her reference to a similar device used by Gabriel Garcia Marquez in *One Hundred Years of Solitude.*
10. Rushdie's view of 'time-as-process' and Saleem's choice of the nature of death may be favourably compared with those of Joyce and Mann. Margaret Church, in her paper in *The Study of Time*, vol. III, ed. J.T. Frazer et. al. (New York: Springer Verlag, 1978) pp. 500-3, says that both these writers "see the circular pattern of lived time as the ultimate reality. They both use the circle to describe process although process itself may be variously interpreted by them." According to her, Mann believes that organic reality "rests on the principle of repetition and recreation, on the circle and the spiral." Church believes that the structure of *The Magic Mountain* supports Mann's "primary belief about the progression of time. Everything in the book moves in circles. Everything returns to its starting point in one way or another. But it is not the closed circle of repetition that Mann celebrates here" for "true human activity is described in spiral form." Mann's hero rejects the 'still centre' of death, of peace and rest, electing instead "the tensions of life, the wind blowing straight in his face, death as part of the life-process, for life feeds on life."
11. Tobin, p. 26

The Politics of Terrorism in Doris Lessing's *The Good Terrorist* and Partap Sharma's *Days of the Turban*

SHYAM S. AGARWALLA

'Kill one, frighten 10,000,' an ancient Chinese proverb, is the best ever definition of terrorism. The lavish media coverage that they receive encourage the perpetrators to believe that they can now frighten ten million.

Are freedom fighters 'terrorists?' Sometimes, yes. "The Scythians" says Richard Clutterbuck, "were probably the earliest terrorists recorded in history (by Herodotus). In 512 B.C. they forced the Persian administration of Darius to withdraw in the face of a scorched earth policy and, one must assume, the terrorization of local officials and collaborators, an early example of nationalist resistance."[1] S.C. Sengupta, for brevity's sake, calls armed revolutionaries "Bengal terrorists,"[2] in India. Dhangopal Mukherjee, in his novel *My Brother's Face,* describes how his elder brother Jadugopal, the revolutionary leader, hoodwinked Intelligence detectives and railwaymen at Howrah station. Later on, influenced by Gandhi, Jadugopal and his fellow-comrades decided to give up the path of violence but not before they had drawn up a treaty (also ratified) with the British Government that "we should be called henceforth Nationalists and not anarchists or terrorists."[3] *Pather Dabi* (The Claim of the Road) is a famous Bengali novel on Indian political revolution, second in importance to Bankimchandra's *Anandmath.* If a message can be gleaned from a novel of stirring incidents and memorable character, it may be thus paraphrased: As one moves along the road of life, one has to meet many claims and realize many values which are more important than political emancipation, but political emancipation must come first, and till it is achieved, everything else is only a diversion.

The difference between Gandhi-ites and their 'terrorist' opponents is most luridly brought out if we compare what a distinguished journalist, an admirer of Mahatma, said with the vitriolic comment made by an imaginary character in Gopal Halder's powerful novel *Ekada*. On the famous Dandi March in 1930, Ramananda Chatterjee, editor of the *Prabasi* and *The Modern Review* prophesied that the spots where Mahatma and his seventy-eight followers would halt would in later times become places of pilgrimage like similar spots mentioned in the *Ramayana* and the *Mahabharata.* From this panegyric we turn to the musings of Amit, the haunted hero of Gopal Halder's *Ekada*: "As Amit contemplated the Dandi March then in full swing, he was reminded of his one-time comrade young Sunil whose path was illuminated by a blinding flash that hides everything else from view. This fervid restless boy, if he heard of the march, would have laughed it away, saying 'Bapuji! Yes, and his battalion of monkeys. The right army for the right general.'" It is by now obvious that the Punjab terrorist, like Sardar Bhagat Singh or the Bengal terrorists like Jadugopal, Binoy, Badal and Dinesh, who believed in the violent overthrow of the British empire in India, were, like the Scythians, nationalists and freedom fighters.

The most vicious terrorists, however, have usually been those motivated by a religion or ideology which convinces them that it is their holy duty to kill to promote their own utopia. After the Second World War, ideological terrorism (Marxist and fascist) got into its stride along with religious fundamentalist and nationalist terrorism. Marxist terrorists in Western Europe were insignificant but they succeeded in Cuba, among Latin American countries, though the final verdict may still be uncertain in El Salvador, Nicaragua and Peru.

ETA (Basque), a minority nationalist group in Spain, has killed about 600 people since 1968. The Irish Revolutionary Army have killed nearly 1,700 but have killed more uninvolved civilians than security forces and businessmen. The Palestine Liberation Organization (PLO) is a nationalist movement without a homeland. Shulamith Hareven, an Israeli Mohammed, gives a real portrait of a PLO terrorist, Mohammad Abu-Nasser:

> Mohammad's way was mapped out for him. At the age of seventeen, he proudly joined a group of George Habash's men. They gave him a hand grenade to throw. They told him he would become a hero, a great man, they kept saying how noble it was to sacrifice yourself for the cause, everyone would admire him. They said they would give him money, support his family, his mother would be proud of him. And he, preening inwardly like a young cock, went to throw the grenade at the queue of soldiers on the road to Jericho, as if he were going to carry out the most glorious deed of his life.[4]

The most sinister aspect of any religious fundamentalism is the technique used—and brilliantly recorded in Granada Television's *Sword of Islam*—to induce in young people the fanatical urge to martyr themselves in the belief that they are serving God through terrorism.

Doris Lessing's *The Good Terrorist* is about "contemporary politics, and ideological utopianism turned to terrorist violence, with her now cosmic, bitingly moral sense of existence."[5] A group of terrorists, calling itself the Communist Centre Union, lives in a squat, a house purchased by the council for redevelopment, and deliberately made uninhabitable to prevent squatters moving in. After due negotiation with the authorities, services are restored, and the group are allowed to live there, rent-free, provided they pay gas and electricity charges and water rates.

The group, as the name shows, is infected with the Marxist ideological bug, believes in utopian plans for violent revolution, including seeking to assist the IRA. Jasper's speech outlines their utopian and ideological plans: "We all know the criminal, the terrible condition of Britain. We all know the fascist imperialist government must be forcibly overthrown. There is no other way forward. The forces that will liberate us are already being forged. We are in the vanguard of these forces, and the responsibility for a glorious future is with us, in our hands."[6] (220) This speech is full of catch phrases strung together by the socialist lexicon and is born out of "his desperate, even ecstatic, seriousness." (220) What are the problems that these revolutionaries have taken in their agenda for discussion? (1) "What trends in the current British scene showed the way to the future? The chosen trends were, one: dissatisfaction over unemployment, "which had to be exploited," two: "the mass disgust of the British people for the Government's policy on nuclear armaments" and, three: "the budding and still unexpressed rejection of the British people for the Tory policy in Northern Ireland." (223) The catch phrase is "the budding and still unexpressed rejection" for their indignation at the Tory policy in Northern Ireland is pure rhetoric, hinged on the Marxist ideology and, unhinged by any concrete action. (2) "The Future of Britain: Full socialism." (223) The atmosphere of the meeting is "heady but comforting." (218) The house, the participants exclaim, has "its comforts, its amenities. More than one, from less well-endowed squats, took a bath at once." (218) The participants are "revellers." (224) Rhetoric and satire make Lessing's *The Good Terrorist* her most savage novel, "as though she has suddenly and finally lost patience with the effort of hoping that the younger generation might build on the painfully learnt political lessons of their elders."[7]

Rhetoric also forms part of Partap Sharma's *Days of the Turban.*[8] Sharma deals with a group of Sikh fanatics or fundamentalists who, under the leadership of Sant Jarnail Singh Bhindranwale, is out to foment disunity and communal disharmony between Sikhs and Hindus, by inventing imaginary and, at times, genuine grievances against "the hindu government." (222) I give below two very interesting and instructive pieces of conversation between Balbir and Amar Singh, a lieutement of the Sant:

> (1) Balbir Sank down on the rug with his knees under him and, faced Amar Singh. "That is not justice, that is communal brutality."
>
> "Ah, Now you see the point. We are teaching the hindu government a lesson."
>
> "But it is not a hindu government. . . ."
>
> "The hindus are in a majority so it ends up being a hindu government."
>
> "What nonsense. The parliament is not composed only of hindus. There are—I don't know how many MPs. . . ."
>
> "Seven hundred and eighty seven. In both houses."
>
> "Right. There are that many members of parliament. Some are muslim, some sikh, some Christian, some parsee—"
>
> "The parsees are zoroastrian. That's the religion."
>
> "Whatever. There are so many of all creeds. And ministers. Ministers are not chosen for their religion but for ability."
>
> Amar Singh gave a scoffing laugh. "Ability and religion. But mainly for the votes of the religious community from which they come."
>
> "There are sikh ministers."
>
> "Puppets. Tools in the hands of the Prime Minister. The Prime Minister is hindu." (222-23)
>
> (2) After a moment of pacing the floor, he [Amar Singh] frowned and murmured, "Has it ever occurred to you that there is no sikh film-star in India? And we have the biggest film industry in the world. Now isn't that discrimination?"
>
> Balbir thought about it. He had to keep at least the spirit of debate going between them. He said: "The film industry is largely Punjabi controlled. Most of the stars are Punjabi. So are the producers and directors. India's film culture is largely based on Punjabi culture. There are plenty of shaven sikhs in the industry."
>
> "Lapsed sikhs, failed sikhs, they are not proper sikhs. A mona is not a sikh. He becomes a hindu." . . .
>
> Amar Singh sighed bitterly. "The film industry portrays us as

> buffoons and clowns. A sikh, to be acceptable, has to be in line with Sardarji jokes. The media discriminates against us. We must change that. That's parts of our demands." (293-94)

These snatches of conversation show two points sharply and clearly. First of all, Amar Singh's "contradictory rigmarole" (204) and unconvincing defence of his deeds are his sincere and genuine attempts "to widen the base of his fanaticism." (204) On the other hand, Balbir is a cool and romantic Naxalite and, therefore, he cannot and does not fall into Amar's wordy mesh. Secondly, and more importantly, in the words of Ruth Whittakar, "The essential quality for any terrorist is lack of imagination, since this would relate violent action to its appalling consequences, and become a deterrent."[9] "Terrorism is a cold act without a shiver." (149)

Alice of *The Good Terrorist* is Balbir of *Days of the Turban* and Jasper is Amar. Jasper and Amar are different from other terrorists of the novels. Alice is the daughter of a rich parent. Her father was the owner of *C. Mellings, Printers and Stationers,* once a "little stationery shop at the back which her father had started in a small way as a trial, and which had become so successful that sometimes he joked it financed everything else." (186-87) Her mother, Dorothy, was rich but Alice and her comrades had sponged off her four years and, now she has had to move into a tiny, ugly flat.

Balbir, the hero of the novel, is a Muhigal Brahmin, born into a clan of fighting Brahmins, peculiar to the Punjab: "And if you, with your sense of history, looked for some traditional justification for such martial behaviour in the thinking caste you might alight, in the past, on the sage Dronacharya who taught the arts of war." (7) Idle, educated, he had "even mixed up for a while with Naxalites. . . . It had seemed an anomaly that Balbir who came from one of the richest houses of the area should espouse the cause of Communist Marxist-Leninist youths. He had even run off to Bihar for a while in order perhaps to probe the origins of his anguish and affiliations. It had taken months to dissuade Balbir of active association." (175-76) All the members of CCU had their urban origin and the Naxalites "were nearly all of urban origin who had no notion of whether it was time for the kharif or the rabi crop." (176)

Alice steals a thousand pounds from her father's firm, bankrupts her mother to feed her comrades, all dreamy revolutionaries, who exploit her and treat her badly. Balbir also steals twenty thousand rupees from his father's account but, unlike Alice, he wants to run away to Europe to follow his glamorous elder brother Raskaan, who has escaped to Europe and become westernized and rich, a businessman in Berlin. Alice entangles herself with CCU out of conviction; Balbir with Uday Singh ('Kumhareya') out of love and with Tarsem out of necessity. If Alice dominates the story of *The Good Terrorist*, Balbir also dominates the story of *Days of the Turban*, the story of terrorism in London and the Punjab.

Jasper is Amar. Both are practical terrorists. If Alice helps Jasper, Balbir helps Uday Singh and, indirectly Amar. What is so extraordinary about Alice, Jasper, Uday and Amar (and indeed, all the terrorists) is their inability to make any connection between cause and effect, action and consequences. Alice tells her mother: "We are going to pull everything down. All of it. This shitty rubbish we live in. It's all coming down. And then you'll see." (330) To execute their cause into action, Alice and her comrades park a car with a time bomb near a hotel: "All down the side of the hotel, it was a scene of disaster; bodies on the pavement, some lying still, some struggling to sit or rise; bits of metal, of shattered glass, handbags, masonry, blood." (355) And even at the final race before planting the bomb, Alice cannot make the final connection between the action and consequences: "Alice was thinking: but people might be killed . . . oh no, that couldn't happen. But inside her chest a pressure was building up, painful like a cry—but she could not let it be heard." (351)

For Uday, murders and bombings are "all political" and the murder of four hindus on the bus is "strategy, tactics, that's all." (51) He "had a genuine commitment, rightly or wrongly, to Bhindranwale's politics. The murders he did commit he did not think of as crimes but as political assassinations, as assignments fulfilled. He did not even know his victims. . . . He did not feel guilty, though he did initially feel revulsion." (43) Amar Singh, like Jasper, is the manager of the terrorist, hiding in the Golden Temple complex. He is also, like Jasper, full of revolutionary ideas. He tells Balbir: "I want you to understand that we're fighting for a cause, and we're fighting because the Congress government won't listen to us. When someone won't listen, what do you do? You make a noise that cannot be ignored. That is what we are doing." (202) For Amar "I act therefore I am. Action is everything." (227) But he, in spite of Balbir's worldly wisdom of the probable intervention of the army in the Golden Temple complex to flush out the terrorists, is unconvinced of the consequences of their terrorist activities and fobs off the advice of Balbir with an illusory picture: "The army cannot enter the Golden Temple complex for the same reason that the police can't. . . . But Mrs. Gandhi won't give the order." (228) It is now a part of history that the army moved into the Golden Temple complex at 22.30 hours on 5 June 1984 and "Balbir never heard of Amar Singh again and was probably right in assuming that he was among those killed and cremated." (380)

In *The Good Terrorist* and *Days of the Turban*, the authors show "how the terrorists keep themselves encapsulated in solipsism, as if aware that knowledge of other people would be a contamination that might infect or dilute their political views."[10]

Doris Lessing, in *The Good Terrorist,* wryly illustrates "how a generalized concern for the masses frequently excludes help or kindness for specific individuals. A lesbian feminist called Frye attacks a desperate, homeless mother and baby who want to join the squat. A frail young man called Philip does most of the essential labour on the house, while the others (apart from Alice) are enjoying themselves on picket lines or demonstrations. He is taken for granted by the commune and dies in an accident because he has lost the will to live. Alice is used by everyone, but takes this as a matter of course. With one or two exceptions, the squatters are selfish and rapacious, and their rhetoric on behalf of the oppressed proletariat is made ludicrous by their own action."[11]

Partap Sharma, in *Days of the Turban*, illustrates the callous attitude of the Punjab terrorists for specific individuals. For instance, they kill "only some Punjabis" (221) for "Autonomy, More power for this state to decide its own future." (221) Uday Singh kills Randhir Sian because "He was against our cause. He mocked it. He was a sikh and yet he mocked it." (148) Sharma comments: "The targets of terrorism are so many, often so unsuspecting, the motivation receding to the infinitesimal point of distant publicity, that the mind sees only numbers, statistics, and a pyramid of blank corpses filed for cremation or mass burial." (149) Amar Singh tortures Uday Singh for eloping with Gulnari, though both loved each other intensely and for that matter, Gulnari goes mad and takes her life away. But, Amar Singh considers this love as misbehaviour, apologizes to Dev Singh, Gulnari's uncle, sends a part of the body of the dead Uday as a gift to Dev Singh.

The actions of Jasper, Alice and their comrades in *The Good Terrorist* and of Amar Singh, Uday Singh and their fellow-fanatics in *Days of the Turban* are inhuman, heart-breaking, lurid and demoniac. Both the novels would have been classed as Gothic Novels but for the fact that Lessing saves hers by the use of irony, humour and vision and Sharma saves his by the age-old Indian ethos and culture of pluralism, tolerance, humour and patience. Both view the terrorists as part of contemporary disease and not a means of curing it. Here, the arts and visions of Lessing and Sharma shine. I sometimes wonder as to why Indian and foreign critics rate Amitav Ghosh, Upamanyu Chatterjee and Bharati Mukherjee higher then Partap Sharma. Is it because each one of them is either a Nirad Chaudhuri or V.S. Naipaul?

NOTES

1. Richard Clutterbuck, "Murder Most Foul," *The Listener*, Vol. 124, 16 August 1990.
2. S.C. Sengupta, *India Wrests Freedom* (Calcutta: Sahitya Sansad, 1982), p. 86.
3. Dhangopal Mukherjee, *My Brother's Face* (New York: E.P. Dutton, 1924), p. 247.
4. Shulamith Hareven, "Portrait of a Terrorist," *London Magazine*, Oct/Nov. 1994, p. 24.
5. Malcolm Bradbury, *The Modern British Novel* (London: Secker and Warburg, 1993), p. 355.
6. Doris Lessing, *The Good Terrorist* (London: Jonathan Cape, 1985).
7. Partap Sharma, *Days of the Turban* (London: The Bodley Head, 1986).
8. Ruth Whittaker, *Doris Lessing* (London: Macmillan, 1988), p. 127.
9. *Ibid.*, p. 128.
10. *Loc. cit.*
11. *Loc. cit.*

Changing Values of Anita Desai's Major Women Characters

M. ADHIKARI

Indian literature, in spite of its variety of language and locale, has found its salvation in the limiting influences of the *Ramayana*, the *Mahabharata* and the *Puranas*. Indian-English literature, despite its Western connections, is intimately related with the traditional Indian psyche. Woman is either a playmate or a bonded labour or a picture of endurance. Occasional sympathetic mythmaking has not reformed the prevalent ideas either in our society or in our literature. Idealistically, a woman is deified but factually, she is exploited socially and sexually. Woman is an object and nothing more.

In Indian fiction, women are the prototypes of the Savitri image and their emotional blackmail continues. The rigid stance of the male writers is intelligible but the endeavour of the women writers of today, to combat the metaphorical decimalization of women's role in literary scripts, is still negligible. Genuine feminine experience and expression are camouflaged, reorganized to follow the norms of ancient precepts. Women seldom revolt against the social injustices, indignities and psychological confinements. Only at very exceptional moments, we do hear the rumblings in their frustrated hearts. Kamala Markandaya's Rukmani (*Nectar in a Sieve*) and Premala (*Some Inner Fury*), lack Candida's effortless assertion of liberty, individuality and superiority. Rukmani's chief concern is to move in the orbit of *pativratas* and her world revolves round her husband's axis. Women in Indian-English fiction, so far, have been either docile and pretty, or, if independent, have sacrificed their endearing qualities. In *Two Virgins,* Lalitha and Saroja opt for two diametrically opposite roles. Lalitha's quest for independence, compels her to embrace a non-conventional way of living. As a result, she soon disappears in the swirling crowd. Not a happy conclusion. Saroja selects the traditional mode and is rewarded. This is the recurring pattern that frequently emerges. Women's tradition-bound experiences are not only applauded but also treated artistically. Markandaya in spite of her strong urge to project an independent woman, fails because she is unwilling to swim against the social and cultural milieu. Here we must mention and congratulate Mahashweta Devi (Bengali), Shivani and Mridula Garg (Hindi) for articulating and presenting women's struggle for equality. The fiction by the modern women novelists of today, is one of the subtlest and complex means of ethical interrogation and utterance to restructure crucial feminine issues through the framework of recent changes in the moral imagination.

Desai while interacting with her readers in a "Meet the Author" programme (arranged by Sahitya Akademi, Delhi) had observed that she was interested in those unusual characters who were ready to go against the tide and had the courage to say "no." She was obviously referring to some of her women protagonists. In her *Where Shall We Go This Summer?* Sita, her protagonist, is found "saying 'no'—but positively, positively saying No. There must be some who say no."[1] Similar ideas were voiced by her when she spoke to Sucheta Mukherji in an informal interview on 4 April 1991: "The characters who go against the grain of society, who try to establish as individuals, I think these are the people that interest me or excite my admiration. . . . Most of them fight against the norm, against what is expected of them. That is why a great many of them stumble and also fail. I don't think the failure is so important. It is the fight they pitch in . . . is important." Desai's conviction has no trace of ambivalence. She considers the fight to be more momentous than the ensuing victory or defeat. But to a woman, a revolt does not come easily as her psyche is structured around different principles. One of these principles, as Jean Baker Miller has propounded, is that women exist to serve other person's needs.[2] Naturally, her dominant role in society is that of a silent giver, healer, sacrificial heifer. Viewing from this angle and comprehending the peculiarity of a woman's psyche, one may perceive changing values of Desai's major women characters.

But what do we mean by values? In a narrow sense, it implies something that is good, desirable and worthwhile; in a wider sense it covers all kinds of rightness, obligation, virtue, truth. To these, some thinkers like D. Ross have added "moral value"[3] and stretched the existing meaning. In literature, while evaluating the role of women, we use the word "values" in the above-mentioned sense. "Moral values" for men and women have different connotations. In relation to men, it simply implies a concern for rules and rights to a more mature sense of responsibility. But for women, the meaning is amended and it changes to concern for others, responsibility, care and obligation.[4] Our society visualizes woman as mother/grandmother, daughter/sister, and wife. Their revolt against the established system or submission before it, is weighted in terms of concern for others, at the cost of the self. The questioning of the paralyzing self-denial by a woman is often considered to be antagonistic to the current concepts of moral values. In spite of these contemporary confining attitudes, a slight shift towards a search for freedom, individual identity etc. can be perceived in Desai's women.

Woman as mother/grandmother is one of the archetypal images of world literature. She is Demeter, Ceres, Astarte, Annapurna, preserving, nourishing, mysteriously reviving, and always self-sacrificing. In contrast to these, Desai's major mother characters are not always the self-effacing types. They enjoy individuality and have a psychological wholeness to reject the dualism rampant in society. It should be profitable to discuss certain examples that prove the argument. Sita of *Where Shall We Go This Summer?*, revolutionizes the concept of motherhood when she refuses to give birth to her child in a cruel, callous world. Seldom is a woman's role in creation considered; she is just the receptacle to hold and shape the master's will. But Sita, anti-normative, unlike her namesake, abandons her husband's house, willingly, not to give birth but to prevent it. This self-imposed exile is the result of her independent thinking. Her desperate cry, "It's not easier, it's harder, harder. It's unbearable," (21) is an expression of fear the that rises in her because of the hostile environment. This fear, finally leads her to the succeeding revolt. She tries to prevent the birth of her child in a destructive society. Monisha's mother in *Voices in the City* is antipodal to the women of her class. Her decision to have a relationship with a man other than her husband, in spite of her children's dislike and opposition, is definitely not conventional. The revolt against her inebriate husband is quite emphatic. The non-conformist behaviour of the mother deconstructs the "enclosure in the patriarchy."[5] The dictates of Manu are ignored with vengeance. Nanda Kaul of *Fire on the Mountain*, apparently a harsh no-nonsense grandmother, resents her daughter's meddling, busy-body ways because she feels threatened by a "noose slipping once more round her neck"[6] of Raka, her great grand-daughter. She refuses to be taken for granted by her daughters, grand-daughters and acquires enough confidence to fend for herself and be self-sufficient. In her character, we again find a confirmation of the fact that Desai's seasoned mothers, resist the traditionally romantic image of a woman. Bim's mother in *Clear Light of Day*[7] is more concerned with her well-being and pleasure of life than her children's. Her role of a mother begins and ends with mere breeding of children. The responsibilities of a mother are shouldered by Mira *Masi*, the foster-mother, a conventional figure. She looks after the children lovingly but "she neither commanded nor chastised and was certainly never obeyed." (111) Her status in the family is that of a respectable maid-servant even though the struggles, strifes and boredom of domestic life find a definition, through her. "She was the tree, she was the soil, she was the earth." (111) Bim realizes much later that the psychologically embedded relationships between Mira *Masi* and the children were never completely satisfying for them. Mira *Masi's* energies were drained by the demands of the family and probably that was the reason of her miserable end. An exploited mother-figure, spirals downward to her death. Desai through Mira *Masi* is writing description rather than prescription. Her implication is clear that women existing within the traditional circle of experience remain non-entities, to be used and wrung dry. Bim in the same novel is presented through triple roles: daughter, sister and mother. She becomes "Bim Masi" for Tara's children. Again and again, we hear the echo of Mira *Masi* in Bim. Her individual struggle features her as a heroic protagonist, admirable but not charming. She (and the readers) can hear Tara's voice "when one is old, one has all kinds of fears, apprehensions." (152) With regret the reader recollects her yesteryear's zest for life and fears that the undermining of her warmth and vigour is due to the burden of circumstances. Though one can bemoan the loss of her endearing qualities yet no sceptic can deny her the credit of emerging as an independent mother figure (for Baba). She can rid herself effortlessly of the props offered by her brother and sister and is different not because she smokes but because she has established her identity.

Desai negates the idea that Maya's (*Cry, the Peacock*) and Monisha's (*Voices in the City*) failure to lead a meaningful life is related merely to their barren condition. Indirectly, she refutes the suggestion that woman's existence sans motherhood is unproductive, worthless and futile. Maya's condescending husband is the symbol of the stifling constrictions of our society. The discernible reader is tempted to question the causes of Monisha's and Maya's tragic end. The ultimate catastrophe is determined not by their sense of deprivation in a childless marriage but their frustrations magnified through a loveless marriage. The first is only an aggravating factor. Women in our society are expected to succeed in life not through their individual efforts but their relationships with men. Since in Maya's and Monisha's case, this relationship never prospers due to a dearth of sympathy and compassion from the men, the novel concludes on a disastrous note. On the whole, at this stage it can be cautiously commented that Desai has desisted from presenting the mature mothers as convention-bound stereotyped characters. Their image has been altered and her memorable mothers/grandmothers are not milchcows to be milched by all and sundry. These etchings are distinctly different from those of R.K.

Narayan or Mulk Raj Anand. But unfortunately, these strong-willed, independent mother characters are neither charming nor adorable. Monisha's liberated mother is anything but imitable. So is Nanda Kaul, the harsh eccentric lady. Not to be emulated in real life. One wonders if Sita should be included in this group. But if one has to accept Desai's statement, Sita too is a protagonist who rebels against the urban ugliness and the stifling world around her. Her pleasing personality emits jarring discordant notes, the moment she decides to revolt, even though she is brought back to the fold subsequently. Desai's women's search for identity is inversely proportioned to their personal pleasantness. The important question is, can Sita be included in this category of independent mothers? Her rebellion melts away on her husband's arrival. "Unwillingly" she feels a "tumult of life and welcome." (*Where Shall We Go This Summer?*, 94) In spite of her suffering under a "non-situation" she cannot but make a compromise. The dice is too heavily loaded against her. Naturally, her revolt turns out to be a farcical experimentation. She realizes that for women the safe way is to stay within the norms of society. Her desire to revolt is not directly portrayed; it is concealed under her over-sensitive and semi-neurotic nature. Is Desai wavering in her conviction or is she merely stating a fact? Bim in *Clear Light of Day*, soon after the demise of her parents, dons the mantle of a mother-figure and from that very instant she becomes increasingly harsh, acrid, exacting, brusque. One can analyze the reasons of this drying process but the fact remains that her metamorphosis is very unnerving. She honestly executes the duties of a mother, preserves her independence, establishes her identity but at what cost? Her definition of the self, as a separate, nonchalant adult, would not be eulogised by many members of our species. But undoubtedly, she demonstrates a definite change in determining the meaning of "values" in relation to women.

Women as daughters/sisters have been frequently painted in Desai's novels. Sisters like Monisha, Tara are still the sacrificing types. Monisha leads a marginal existence in the shadow of men but Bim's achievement as a college teacher, soon gives her social recognition. In spite of it, her sacrifices are appreciated by her sister Tara only. Others either ignore it or take it for granted. During her childhood days, she is a tomboyish girl, playing tricks happily on others, along with her brother Raja. Since the direct parental control is little, she never feels inferior to her brother, for being a girl. Much later in the story, while sharing her secret thoughts, the reader becomes aware of her grudge against Raja for not sharing the family responsibility equitably. Bim's values of life, in her quest for autonomy, had undergone a sea-change but by following the concept of "caring" and "shouldering the responsibility," she remains tradition-bound. Monisha's status as a *persona non grata* does not change in spite of her knowledge of French, Russian and Kafka. She never enjoys the liberties that Bim does. Her protective feeling for Nirode, her brother, is so intense and maternal that she "suffers his fever deeply because it is hers."[8] She is aware of the "cages" and "bars" of her life and thus wishes to set Nirode free. His one-dimensional existence, she wishes to compensate by sharing his humiliations. Monisha is the Indian version of Antigone, an archetype. Her sister Amla, is poles apart. Monisha's last instruction to Amla, "Amla always go in opposite direction," (160) is not only her way of revolt against the dehumanizing ways of the society but also a request to change and frame a particular consciousness and ethic that she had failed to do. Her transition from silence to speech is unfortunately too short-lived. Amla, on the other hand, feels only a few pangs of conscience for not sharing the family load. Her values, now altered, make her regret dereliction of duty yet she has acquired enough courage to disapprove of Monisha's marriage with a callous man: "How unfair, how criminally unfair." (199) She follows her own career and boldly faces the oppositions coming from different quarters. Tara (*Clear Light of Day*) is quite unlike Amla. She orbits around her husband and children and remains passively worked up with the problems of her brother and sister. As a sister, she is non-interested but as a chaste wife of an aggressive intelligent husband, she is caring and responsible. The feeling of being pushed by her family members surfaces only on rare, depressed moments. Following her husband, always a "strain," had "drained" her. (18) Frequently or occasionally, pricks of conscience are to be found in women only. Men are blissfully unaware of their shortcomings. Raja, Nirode, Jiban, Bakul, etc. can turn a blind eye to the justified demands of the women in their family. They are privileged to preserve their self-interest. Thus thematically, Desai hesitantly negates the age-old values celebrated in our society. It is not that one would expect Desai to sketch selfish sisters but one would definitely like her to draw occasionally, men who would share the burden of life fairly. In the patriarchal society, probably, her hands are bound by realism.

Surprisingly enough, Desai's protagonists as daughters, against Shashi Deshpande's girl-child (*That Long Silence*), enjoy reasonably happy adolescent years. Maya is very happy in her childhood, being the cynosure of her father's eye; Sita's memories of young days are sour but her clear awareness of discrimination comes much later. Bim has no experience of child oppression as she is always equal to Raja; docile Tara has a normal childhood under the protective tree of Mira *Masi;* Sara

(*Bye-Bye Blackbird*), in spite of her conservative family, remains happy as she is not discredited for being a girl; Monisha and Amla share the ups and downs of a child's life along with Nirode; Leela, of *Village by the Sea* shares the joys and sorrows of life with her brother. On the whole, women as daughters remain quite satisfied though often over-protected. Amla emerges as a woman of substance; she resolves her problems neither through marriage nor death; escapes the time-worn mould of an ever-dutiful, unselfish woman, conventionally applauded for breathing the rarefied air of self-denial.

Desai in her novels has concentrated more on the urban middle-class married woman than anything else. Career-minded spinsters are few and far between though we do meet Bim and Amla. Sara (*Bye-Bye Blackbird*), in spite of her western upbringing is domesticated, docile, duty-bound, timid like a typical "Bengali girl." She seldom defies or is infuriated by the dominating and often too demanding instructions of her Indian husband. Willingly, she decides to migrate to India as an Indian wife. Even in her hours of loneliness, self-awareness, nothing seems to boil in her. Her surrender to the traditional image of an Indian daughter-in-law and wife is partly due to her genuine love for her husband and partly due to her fear of being deserted by him and consequently ostracized by society. This insecurity and the pressures of social stigma are the causes of her dramatic decision. Not all is the result of an *affair de coeur*. In contrast, Maya's (*Cry, the Peacock*) presentation as an Indian wife, is antithetical to the Sita-image. Her isolation, the mundane existence and the feeling of boredom is common to most of the Indian wives but her fight to negate the physical and psychological vacuum, give her a positive distinction. She articulates the disappointments of her love-life and we track her internal and external thought-process. In a neurotic state, she becomes convinced of her husband's detachment and kills him. I feel here, Desai has attempted to project a woman's fight for individuality and liberation. Her desire to be met half-way, is not unjustified yet such considerations cannot be expected from the lord of the household. Along with Maya, the reader regrets that had it been so, "all might have been quite different."[9] Maya's loss of mental moorings, an archetypal situation is caused by her sensitive nature and her refusal to make a compromise with her dumb existence. No doubt her reactions are violent but who can forget that the societal pressures are responsible for her lunacy? In the closing section of the novel, she topples from the roof of the house and does not commit suicide as is often believed. She had never desired to resolve her personal problems through death. In her fear-clouded mind, she perceives the approach of her mother-in-law, an attempt to confine and subdue her. She reacts, and in the ensuring scuffle the tragic end is brought about. Desai in the course of different interviews had often reiterated that Sita's 'No' is very emphatic. But in my opinion, Maya's non-acceptance of the limiting relationships, is more declaratory. In her rational state, she rightly feels that her individuality and identity are being threatened, even though she is born and brought up in a conservative atmosphere. For her tradition-bound in-laws, her demands are unconventional and quite disturbing. She revolts against the mundane domesticity. Her modified version of "values" had changed the meaning of life. It was no longer a mere gratification of the physical self. Monisha's problem is quite different. As a truly Indian wife, she seldom has the courage to oppose her husband, even for a just cause. Her craving for her husband's company is smothered too often, too easily. Infrequently and half-heartedly, she attempts to wrench her right. All her education and refinement cannot save her from the self-sought disaster. She paradoxically chooses death as a fulfilling reaction. Her docile nature seals her fate. Bereft of the little spark of courage, she is never inspired to say "no." Amla her outspoken assertive sister, may have regrets but she never permits others to meddle in her affairs. Learning through trial and error, she follows her own inclinations. A representative of the modern up-coming young generation, she is ready to challenge the ancient value-system of "double standards."

Sita's modernity is ironically submerged in her conformable name. A cursory glance reveals that her attempts to define herself and to suspend the process of annihilation, lack in tenacity. She is made to "adjust" with her prudent husband because of the pressures of the institutionalized society. Women are disciplined to follow the traditional values to absorb the feelings of inferiority and dependence. For Sita, "It was over." (*Where Shall We Go This Summer?*, 110) Should one feel happy for her fruitless efforts? Desai's views, as mentioned earlier, are very emphatic on this point. According to her the psychology to resist and revolt is more important than the final result.

The above analysis should conclusively assist us to draw certain inferences. Desai's mature mothers are undoubtedly very confident; their demand for personal identity is strikingly pronounced; their will to question the established value-system is clearly demonstrated; they have won their liberty but lost their charming personality. Young mothers and wives are still fledglings, learning to free themselves from the constraining clutches of society. To make a success of their family life, they remain trapped between life and death. Frequently, Monisha's, Sita's and Maya's search for personal identity, ends in the fragmentation of their personality. The tussle between the ideal and the real is still too severe for them to bear. Sara's survival is linked with her surrender to the old value system. Amla goes in search of new horizons but remains apologetic about her career-mindedness. Quite differently, she asserts her personality. Along with these memorable protagonists one need not discuss the very sketchy women characters of *In Custody* (Begum Imtiaz and Sarla) and *Baumgartner's Bombay* (Lotte). These mainstream novels revolve round the lives of men, and the women characters are mere appendages only.

On the whole one can say that Desai is moving very cautiously towards the creation of self-conscious women characters. She is yet to take the plunge to create the staunch believers of the new value system who can dare to question the established norms, degrading to women. Her task is difficult because a woman's psyche is governed by different principles and she has to create "probable" characters. Desai's Indian upbringing also might be causing certain problems. Her women continue to be second class citizens of our society. Yet one cannot overlook her achievement as she has made women aware of man's unjust stance. The new woman is in her embryonic stage and one can hope to see her birth in Anita Desai's new imaginative efforts.

NOTES

1. (Delhi: Vikas, 1975), p. 108.
2. *Toward a New Psychology of Women* (2nd ed., Boston: Beacon Press, 1986), pp. 62.
3. *The Encyclopedia of Philosophy*, ed. Paul Edwards (New York: Macmillan and the Free Press, 1967), Vol. 8, p. 230.
4. Carol Macmillan, *In a Different Voice: Psychological Theory and Women's Voice* (Cambridge: Harvard University Press, 1982), p. 17.
5. Annis Pratt, *Archetypal Patterns in Women's Fiction* (Bloomington: Indiana University Press, 1981), p. 40.
6. Anita Desai, *Fire on the Mountain* (New Delhi: Allied, 1977), p. 19.
7. Anita Desai, *Clear Light of Day* (New Delhi: Allied, 1980).
8. Anita Desai, *Voices in the City* (London: Peter Owen, 1965), p. 130.
9. Anita Desai, *Cry the Peacock* (New Delhi: Orient Paperback, 1980), p. 198.

Art, Matter and Spirit: Kamala Markandaya's *Possession*

JYOTSNA SAHU

Every great work of art reveals a confrontation between spirit and matter. It is born of this confrontation, without any commitment. It leaves the readers and viewers with tension. The readers or the viewers strive to lessen the tension by making an attempt to shorten the distance between the readers, writers and the work. The readers from this world can alone enter the world of imagination through a sympathetic understanding or what is called empathy. Nevertheless, there remains a twilight zone between the artist and the readers. Every great work of art leaves with that twilight zone to be lighted by readers from generation to generation.

Kamala Markandaya's *Possession*[1] leaves the readers with that twilight zone to be lighted. This paper will be an attempt to fathom that twilight zone where Art, Matter and Spirit confront, and not coalesce.

Art is neither whole matter nor whole spirit. It accepts both the worlds, but belongs to its own world. In the words of Sri Aurobindo, "All art starts from the sensuous and sensible, or takes it as a continual point of reference or, at the lowest, uses it as a symbol and a fount of images; even when it soars into invisible words, it is from the earth that it soars; but equally all art worth the name must go beyond the visible, must reveal, must show us something that is hidden, and in its total effect not reproduce but create."[2]

Markandaya's *Possession* is based on the predicament of an artist and his art. An artist like his art is a free spirit. Any attempt to possess him is to put an end to his art. Markandaya's *Possession* is the story of Valmiki, shortened as Val, a born artist. He is a prodigy who paints on the mud wall of his village in Tamilnadu with the help of charcoal. He paints whatever comes to his heart. Caroline is awestruck to see this young prodigy painting.

Caroline gives a form to his art. She brings this "mute Milton" to the limelight. Caroline had come to a remote village of Tamilnadu in search of Arak, was herself intoxicated by the charcoal drawing in the mud wall of this prodigious child. She forgot all about 'Arak' and got interested in the child's art that was considered a luxury in Val's home where two times food was a dream. Val, the "Useless on the land, useless at home" proved a priceless possession for Caroline. (27) But she did not know the depth of his character. He was formless, belonged to the dark world of cave from where all creation begins. But Caroline with her vanity and intellectual aristocracy failed to fathom the depth and intensity of that unknown, fathomless world. It is the world of divine otherness. The world where spirit and matter do not coalesce, but play a simultaneous role in bringing out the art to the limelight. It is a spiritual world, beyond the ethical, moral world of ours. In this world Caroline's presence is as much responsible as Swami's. What Swami knew, Caroline did not. Val's painting on the mud wall with a charcoal is what the primitive artist used to do who had no exposure, and when the light of civilization had not dawned. Caroline was interested in the boy who was a goatherd and who had no idea of what he was doing. What he did was to amuse himself in his lonely moments. He did what the muse whispered to his heart. In the words of Caroline, "He paints. He's got nothing, of anything that he ought to have, but he can paint." (9) He listened to the unintelligible, unspoken words of his heart which Swami never tried to interfere. Caroline from the beginning wanted to possess the child-artist, wanted to give a form to his art by giving him exposure to the world of art, the colour, the brush, the chisel a world which gives importance to these things. He was possessed by Caroline. Caroline said "That is how much *arak* meant to me. But the boy's real. I'm not going to let him throw himself away here." (11) Caroline thought him "wasted" (10) in the village. She took him to London; exposed him to the modern world where Val took time to acclimatize; and Caroline always held him under her arm: "She put her arm around the boy, as it were taking possession of him in full view of his family." (20)

Although Caroline gave a form to Val's art she failed to understand the tragic tension in the artist. The tension in an artist lies when he fails to give form and expression to his innermost thought. The artist always feels the inadequacy in him, he has the feeling that something remains to be spoken. Every attempt of the artist is, to quote Eliot, "A holy new start, and a different kind of failure." The brush and chisel are not enough to express the innermost thought of an artist. He needs new experience. Val was grateful to Caroline. It was she who, in fact, was responsible for his rise, his popularity. But Val never cared for his popularity, he was essentially a loner. Caroline's intimacy and too much passion for possession sometimes brought Val a kind of rebellion. Every artist according to Albert Camus, is a "Rebel." But there was no room available to Val to rebel. He got the outlet through Ellie. Sex very often can act as a tranquillizer against the rebellious spirit. Ellie with her youth offered a new experience for Val: "She had been his inspiration, his model, his success was at least partly hers." (123) He drew the nude body of Ellie with all his experience and intense feeling. What Ellie offered to Val, Caroline feared losing the hold on Val: "Caroline and Valmiki continued to sleep in the same bed at night." (199) She too wanted to have sex with Val. So Caroline stood as a stumbling block to their intimacy. This resulted in the death of Ellie: she committed suicide. This separation also affected the creation of Val. He became restless; started hating Caroline. His affair with Ellie also affected his relationship with Annabel. Annabel disgracefully left him, when she came to know the sad story of Ellie: "Annabel frightened, confused, was groping for the terrible truth, the unfinished truth that Caroline had hung in the air." (206) All these experiences affected the artist. He failed to regain his equilibrium until Swami's sudden appearance in London which appears very improbable. Metaphorically Swami represents this spirit whereas Caroline, Ellie, Annabel and Val's life in London are the experiences of the material world. An artist needs the experiences of both the worlds: the world of the spirit and the world of the senses or what Germans would call "Guist" and "Nature." An artist needs to understand both the worlds, *Vita Activa* and *Vita Contemplativa.* Art captures the romance of living, but at the same time it is larger than life.

NOTES

1. Kamala Markandaya, *Possession* (Bombay: Jaico, 1967).
2. Sri Aurobindo, *Birth Centenary Literary,* Vol. 9, p. 5.

Symbolism in Markandaya's *Two Virgins*

RAMESH K. SRIVASTAVA

One reason for the adverse critical reception of Kamala Markandaya's *Two Virgins* is the novel's being so heavily loaded with symbols and skin-deep connections that the characters and incidents appear as mere flag-bearers of the novelist's ideas. In order to depict various characters and their evolving personalities, Markandaya makes use of a series of symbols and images which are from birds and animals, living and lifeless objects, such as, mouse, dove, eagle, butterfly, bats, wood, etc. As if to further clarify her obvious intentions, she refers in the novel to the story of "a town mouse and a country mouse" originally narrated by Miss Mendoza to Lalitha who, now in her turn, narrates it to her sister Saroja: "The town mouse visiting his country cousin had lamented the loss of his town comforts while enjoying what the country had to offer, while on a return visit it had been the other way round."[1] This simple fable characterizes the lifestyles of Lalitha and Saroja—one becoming identified with the town mouse while the other with the country mouse.

Lalitha obviously can be associated with, what Miss Mendoza calls, "a town itself, Lalitha represents external beauty in contrast to Manikkam's wife whose beauty consists in her benevolent activities. Lalitha is so much intoxicated with the idea of urban life that she considers her village house as primitive and barbaric in the absence of a refrigerator and a phone. With her superficial knowledge of the city, Lalitha symbolizes the modern youths who glorify the urban life and ultimately become its prey. Margaret Joseph considers her "a symbol of the social forces that drive modern youth to the magnetic city."[2] A.V. Krishna Rao feels that Lalitha symbolizes "the impetuosity of the youth."[3] Lalitha is captivated by Miss Mendoza's modern ways—her manner of sitting in chairs, and her use of forks and spoons in taking meals. Unlike her crumpled-looking rural sister Saroja, Lalitha wishes to appear flower-fresh all the time. Besides being crazy for slimness, she spends hours to bathe and braid her hair, piles her tresses in a new style and exhibits her phenomenal eyelashes. She prefers English to Indian dance.

Typical of modern youths educated in public schools, Lalitha begins to criticize the Indian religion and culture in an attempt to prove her liberal attitude to life. By comparing Lachu's act of dallying with girls with that of Lord Krishna, she exposes her shallow ideas infected in her mind by Christian Mission School wherein Indian gods and goddesses were often spoken of disparagingly. She also talks of the resurrection of Manikkam's dead child as opposed to the Hindu view of transmigration of its soul.

Convinced that her soul belongs to the city, Lalitha derisively terms her backward village as a one-horse town, and an outpost of civilization having a primitive life. She tells Aunt Alamelu, "your day, dear Aunt, is as dead as the dodo." (127) Deciding to leave the village, Lalitha takes to the path of suicide well and subsequently falls into a bog surrounding the well. The incident symbolizes the pitfalls and dangers that a rural-born person posing to be a "town mouse" confronts when she leaves her protected home. Caked in mud and badly soiled due to her fall, she is cleaned with water by Appa, and Amma—her father and mother—and their cleansing exercise becomes symbolic of their subsequent act of decently covering up the entire abortion affair after Lalitha comes back pregnant and spoiled from the city. The entire urban world is a bog into which a rural virgin like Lalitha is bound to fall the moment she ventures out of her protected limits.

The other symbols which have been used in relation to the various stages in the evolution of Lalitha are the butterfly, the dove, and the eagle. In the first stage, Lalitha's feelings are symbolized by a dove and a butterfly, the common traits of which are innocence, purity, beauty and dreaminess. Lalitha has her dove-like innocence, is beautiful as a butterfly and a certain amount of flitting modernity characterizes her. For C.G. Jung, "The butterfly is a symbol and allegory of the psyche"4 and here it is of Lalitha's psyche. The idea finds support in Tom Chetwynd who thinks that the butterfly represents one of the functions of psyche as well as "a symbol of growth and transformation of psyche."5 Furthermore, the evolution of a butterfly from a caterpillar symbolizes "the transition from physical, earthbound sensation to the flight of the mind experienced inwardly."6 A dove signifies the quality of being soft, smooth and gentleness of the feminine in nature. The symbols usually refer to the inner reality, particularly so when adjectives are not specifically mentioned. Chetwynd writes: "The image of the bird is a reflection of the thoughts, fantasies and symbols which dwell in the upper regions; it is a representation of those symbolic flights of fancy which carry man into the realms of the unconscious." (49) The qualities of the birds suggest which aspect of the mind's content is being symbolized. The eagle suggests the bright, conscious and positive side. Dove, in particular, has "the attribute of the Love Goddess as well as the Holy Spirit. This is the Archetype of Relationships and values which arise from feeling. The union of distinct, individual entities."[7] Lalitha's belief that she is meant for a place far superior to the village, that she has beauty that equips her to become a film actress, and that she has a dreamy, romantic temperament that urges her to find a lover in Mr. Gupta, the film producer, are reflected in these images. When she expresses her desire to be an actress, even when opposed by Aunt Alamelu, Lalitha feels "like a dove on the wing" and that she "could soar away, away, like an eagle to the topmost peak of the sacred mountain." (106) She considers the city and the acting as "heaven" and to look beautiful "worth all the trouble in the world." (132) She flitted gracefully butterfly-like from place to place, creating new dance patterns as if she were with some other bats or birds. She executed a *colam* pattern in saffron and white and designated "a dove on a trellis in a garden." (106) The trellis and the garden were common but Lalitha had added the dove to them. Mr. Gupta's act of blurring the dove by carelessly shuffling his feet symbolizes his act of deflowering Lalitha of her virginity and dove-like purity.

Lalitha's subsequent drawing of an eagle after the dove was blurred away by Mr. Gupta's shuffling feet symbolizes the second stage in her transformation from innocence to experience, and from simplicity to aggressive nature. Commenting on this transformation, Madhusudan Prasad writes that the "dove-like Lalitha loses her purity and grows ambitious like an eagle."[8] In Anand's novel *The Old Woman and the Cow,* Gauri initially becomes a symbol of cow but after being troubled by her husband Panchi and her mother-in-law Kesaro, she subsequently becomes a tigress. An eagle can soar high in the sky, look down upon the puny, earth-bound creatures and can swoop down anywhere at will. It has the capability not only of protecting itself but of launching an offensive against others if need be. It is natural that Lalitha, brimming with self-confidence, explains to Saroja that the eagle represents her as well as her ambitions. She reveals too the secrets of sexual pleasure to Saroja, and her romantic life with Mr. Gupta which culminate in her abortion. In her pregnant state, she becomes a strayed heifer but who, after abortion, looked "like burnt-out wood; only just holding her shape." (220) Since Lalitha is associated with the butterfly, Mr. Gupta can be with the bats. The description given in the novel becomes quite symbolic: "The bats were after the butterflies, which were dying, whose day was over. They fluttered their wings feebly, were seized, were finished." (229) Saroja, treading on Lalitha's footsteps, becomes attracted to Devraj though she is saved from being exploited by him. Thus both Gupta and Devraj are the bats chasing butterflies named Lalitha and Saroja. Margaret Joseph writes: "Butterflies are easily linked with pretty girls, and the bats that destroy the butterflies with city slickers like Gupta." (201) Lalitha, who was exquisitely fashioned, "demanded beauty and perfection out of life" but who like a spoiled butterfly after abortion lay half-dead in darkness "like felled timber." (230) She looked coarse and ugly; the lily quality of her was gone.

Saroja symbolizes the dewy freshness and innocence of village life, gradually withering in the aftermath of India's rapid industrialization. She looks yearningly to the city and to the West, has a taste of urban life, but feeling disappointed, she comes back to her rural life, where lay real happiness for her—all else being ephemeral. Because of her living in the village, she has a healthy attitude to life, and believes life to be long and colourful "like a shining ribbon, yards and yards of it coming abundantly off a heavenly blue spool." (57)

Saroja can be considered "a country mouse." (193) Having rural habits and tastes, Saroja has ambitions befitting only rural women, such as, having lovely cuddly babies, or like wishing to be rounded and curvy rather than slim. When she takes deep breaths to inhale tender vapours and odours emanating from the earth after the rains, Miss Mendoza calls her the "child of the soil." (97) Saroja has beauty but not that polish which could find appreciation in the eyes of the city people. She is timid, has conscience and is considerate to others, including animals—something that Lalitha lacks. Buffaloes obeyed her but resisted Lalitha. Being rural oriented, Saroja opposes the introduction of machines in the village. In the beginning, she had no knowledge of the town beyond a faint recollection of what someone had commented that in town it was "a bit of a thieves' kitchen . . . you have to have your wits about you." (54) She noticed some kind of hardness on the faces of city boys she had not seen in the village.

Being unaware of the city noise, the activity and the bustle, Saroja disapproves of the crammed way of the town without open spaces or greenery but with brick and cement buildings. She is also conscious that the village cannot remain permanently insulated from urban influence and that their innocence and virginity could be spoiled by the acid touch of the city through movies and other influences. In the beginning, she failed to understand what a packet of condoms was meant for, but realizes the implication of illicit relations when she notices dozens of unmarried girls with babies in the village. In the city, Lalitha appeared so much to shake the stream of her life that even Saroja herself was momentarily charmed by Devraj and wanted to fling herself into his arms. But she continues to win the confidence of her mother who prides in Saroja's innocence and her act of brushing in contrast to Lalitha's shamelessness. After staying in the city for sometime, Saroja hated it and wanted to go home in the village. K.S. Ramamurti considers Saroja "a symbol of a healthy reconciliation of two different attitudes to life."[9]

Appa and Rangu can be associated with the river which comes up from the mountain and moves impetuously overcoming all hurdles and obstacles towards freedom in order to merge itself with the Ocean where other rivers fall. Appa symbolizes that spirit of freedom in which impediments are thrown away. When India was under the colonial rule of the British, Appa and Rangu fought and suffered for its freedom. Appa had printed pamphlets for which his house was burnt while Rangu was beaten up and killed. In his general attitude to life, Appa becomes a symbol of the rational individualist and lover of the country but without its closed-door culture. He becomes an advocate for an open-minded society and a spokesman of Markandaya.

In contrast to Appa, Amma is religious-minded, somewhat orthodox and even superstitious in a material world where religious feelings are shrinking very fast. Her position and plight is symbolized by the *tulasi* plant, the shrine and the prayer room. Amma's praying was ritualistic—"a reverent mumbling," as a part of the Hindu tradition and not emanating from her soul—because she had copied it from Sanskrit. She has all praise for Sita's purity and her unwavering devotion to Rama. In her view, Mr. Gupta was responsible for Lalitha's pregnancy. She admires Miss Mendoza for running her school well, for teaching lovely things to Lalitha, but not for leading an unmarried life. Kind-hearted as she is, she cannot bear the pain of the injured monkey who becomes identified with her children, particularly with Lalitha, after she suffers in the city at the hands of Mr. Gupta.

Appa's family with Aunt Alamelu symbolizes the disintegrating joint-family system which is outdated, anachronistic and good-for-nothing. Aunt Alamelu belongs to the older generation which believes in Fate and in traditional wisdom. She does all the work but being a widow has no status in the family or society. For Appa, she is an "old meddling bag," for Saroja, "behind the times"; for Lalitha, "positively antediluvian"; and for herself, she is less than dust. K.S. Ramamurti considers her "a symbol of tradition." (206)

Aunt Alamelu disapproves of Miss Mendoza's "modern" ways which Lalitha terms "Cosmopolitan." She is opposed to the girls riding bicycles or associating themselves with people below their class. She opposes Lalitha's acting in films on the ground that a girl from a respectable family is not supposed to act like a devadasi and that no one in their family for twenty generations had ever done such a thing. It was shameful, without any propriety, "totally contrary to the code of our Hindu decorum which has safeguarded the virtue of our youth for a thousand years." (176) In her view, the girls must be kept in complete obedience within four walls of the house if they are not to be spoiled which is what the sense of freedom does. Aunt Alamelu opposes Appa's talk of the rights of children which had led to Lalitha's corruption, saying "you have given your children rights and they have come home to roost" (177) as also his proposal to take Saroja to the city, saying, "you're putting virgins in a whorehouse." (180)

Miss Mendoza, with her English shoes, well-stitched clothes, sophisticated manners and a sense of superiority symbolizes the Western culture which has infected the mind of Indian youth. As the Englishmen claimed to have civilized Indians, she believes that the missionary school gave not only artistic opportunities to its students but also developed the character of the girls. However, as Indians knew then the pragmatic nature of the British colonizers behind the altruistic facade they maintained, so do Appa and Aunt Alamelu know about Miss Mendoza who is derisively called "that three-rupee convert" because her ancestors had embraced Christianity on receiving payments at the rate of three rupees per person. Aunt Alamelu satirizes her as "that strutting peahen with the fancy notions" for putting ideas into Lalitha's head while Appa blames her pernicious influence for Lalitha's fall. Miss Mendoza shows her sense of superiority in humbling Appa by sanctioning funds from her school for Lalitha's trip to go to the city for viewing films. She stands up symbolically straighter than usual and crushes Appa the same way as the British rule had suppressed nationalists and national culture. Appa feels humiliated on realization that being poor he could not manage the money for his daughter's trip. Sanctioning funds to his Lalitha could be equated with the loans being sanctioned by the West to India at the cost of its self-respect.

Mr. Gupta too is modern and has immense impact on Lalitha. For Margaret Joseph, he becomes "a symbol of Western materialism corrupting rural values." (148) For A.V. Krishna Rao, Mr. Gupta "symbolizes the fast-changing, superficial and immoral exploiting system of the city." (21) To Lalitha, he appeared as attractive as a "man from another planet." The incident of Mr. Gupta's car being taken out of the bog by a team of two bullocks and a dozen men implies that whenever the citymen are caught in a mess, as were Lalitha and Mr. Gupta, it is the village people who come to their rescue. Symbolically, Chetwynd writes, the bog could be associated with the earth which was initially a ball of fiery mud. A modern man is hardly capable of grasping "his precarious position semi-stuck to a big ball of fiery mud, spinning through endless space and time." (107) Mr. Gupta and Lalitha symbolize modern men and women who madly run after materialistic comforts and sensuous pleasures only to be bogged down in spiritual wasteland. The car is an indisputed symbol of urban life as the bullock cart is that of the village. Appa and Amma save Mr. Gupta by not filing against him a criminal complaint of seducing their daughter Lalitha, and by agreeing for her abortion. For Aunt Alamelu, Lalitha's pregnancy was the mud thrown at the girl a part of which was bound to stick to the family. This idea gets further reinforced by the grapevine at Mr. Gupta's place which has grapes coated with the city dust as if to show what defiles nature's purity.

Manikkam, a poor milkman, with an unmanageably large number of children, "symbolizes the poverty of a large family."[10] He wanted to sell the barren cow to a butcher for some money but his wife, being a kind-hearted Hindu woman, would not agree to cow-slaughter: "should I grudge her a mouthful of grass after all the milk that has flowed from her these past years?" (6) Being a wet-nurse, Manikkam's wife suckled others' babies along with her own, including of those women who did not want to spoil their shapely breasts which suckling did. It is probably poverty that makes Manikkam frustrated and cruel as reflected in his act of giving an old cow to the butcher and of stoning the monkeys on the tamarind tree.

The injured monkey symbolizes a cripple who is not welcome in the tribe whether of animals or of human beings. His mother obviously intended it to die when she abandoned it because the tribe could not accept a cripple, even if it could tolerate one. Chingleput too had a crippled foot. Saroja wondered if Chingleput's mother too had intended him to die when she had abandoned him and considered society to be criminal whether it was of monkeys or of human beings. The wooden beam too can be taken as a symbol of society—solid from outside but hollowed and eaten up from within. If the crows with their bright beady eyes could have the corn off the cobs, making them as stark as lingam, white ants eat up and hollow the beam from inside. The beam which was to be hoisted up for the buffalo shed was light and hollow: "The eaten up beam lay around for weeks. It kept its shape, but it was crumbling and hollow inside. White ants scuffled in and out of the tunnels, with wood crumbs in their jaws. Saroja knew they ate wood but it never ceased to surprise her." (23)

Enumerating the symbols in *Two Virgins* appears to be—and is—a mechanical exercise since Markandaya has not used the sophisticated method of employment as she had in her earlier novels. A good use of symbols is like an act of generosity which is best left to be understood and never to be explicitly stated. While commenting on his own use of symbols, Ernest Hemingway writes: "The dignity of movement of an iceberg is due to only one-eighth of its being above water,"[11] and implicitly the dignity of symbols lay in being intangible. Kamala Markandaya, usually adept in employing symbols in her other novels, uses them here almost contrary to Hemingway's iceberg principle, because the symbols are quite obvious and glaringly stick out in the text of the novel. In an interview with Robert Manning, Hemingway criticized the unhealthy trend of embedding predetermined symbols in a work of art: "No good book has ever been written that has in it symbols arrived at before hand and stuck in." He took a piece of French bread and said, "That kind of symbol sticks out like—like raisins in raisin bread. Raisin bread is all right, but plain bread is better."[12] The symbols that are too easy to make out lose their charm for a critic or a reader by denying him the pleasure of delightfully discovering them. This way Markandaya's *Two Virgins* becomes a feast of symbols, not of enigmatic rural delicacies whose tastes a diner discovers through his palate, but of neatly arranged cook-book dishes with tell-tale name-tags perched before them; they may satisfy the hunger but starve the soul.

NOTES

1. *Two Virgins* (1974; rpt. New Delhi: Vikas, 1977), p. 193.
2. Margaret Joseph, *Kamala Markandaya* (New Delhi: Arnold-Heinemann, 1980), pp. 146-47.
3. "Continuity and Change in the Novels of Kamala Markandaya" in *Perspectives on Kamala Markandaya,* ed. Madhusudan Prasad (Ghaziabad: Vimal, 1984), p. 21.
4. *Symbols of Transformation* (London: Routledge and Kegan Paul, 1956), p. 250.
5. *A Dictionary of Symbols* (London: Paladin, 1982), p. 403.
6. *Ibid.,* p. 404.
7. *Ibid.,* p. 51.
8. "Introduction," *Perspectives,* p. xxviii.
9. "*Two Virgins:* A Problem Novel," *Perspectives,* p. 206.
10. Margaret Joseph, pp. 147-48.
11. *Green Hills of Africa* (New York: Charles Scribner's, 1932), p. 192.
12. "Hemingway in Cuba," *Atlantic Monthly,* 216 (Aug. 1965), p. 104.

Cultural and Political Allegory in Nayantara Sahgal's *Rich Like Us*

MAKARAND PARANJAPE

Nayantara Sahgal's *Rich Like Us* is her most ambitious and complex novel. Its importance, both artistic and political, was recognized in its being awarded the Sinclair Prize for fiction and the Indian Sahitya Akademi award for the best book in English for the year 1986. It is also the key novel to consider if we are examining how women characters respond to the tradition; it is also the most radical of her novels politically. Finally, with *Rich Like Us* Sahgal properly enters the fictional domain of post-modernism. From the more or less straight narratives of the past in which the fictional mode might be termed mimetic, Sahgal uses symbolism and allegory extensively in *Rich Like Us*. The earlier novels are, formally, somewhat dull and stodgy; they are boring in an upper-class, well-bred, genteel, "club" manner. But *Rich Like Us* attempts at an adventureness in form which is both challenging and refreshing.

So far as the narrative shift is concerned, *The Day in Shadow* marks the end of one phase. *A Situation in New Delhi* is a transitional novel in which the narrative becomes clipped and elliptical, the closure uncertain and abrupt. Sahgal has moved into new pastures formally. But the real breakthrough occurs, as I shall show, in *Rich Like Us*.

Critics have pointed out how the concern with women's issues is naive in the earlier novels, acquiring a complexity only in *Rich Like Us*. There have also been attempts to suggest a break between the earlier women and Sonali. It is argued the earlier women are essentially drifters, while the later ones are actors, taking the initiative to change their lives. Actually, I don't see such a break. There is, as Jasbir Jain says, a gradual evolution from the earlier to later ones.[1] Sonali is a type of Rashmi, Saroj, or Simrit. Their values are similar. The only difference is that Sonali is more self-aware and self-assured.

Thematically, then, I don't see a break in Sahgal's work in the middle phase. There is a fullness of harmony and realization as early as *Storm in Chandigarh*. In this significant novel, I find a clear articulation of not only Sahgal's values, but also of her solutions to the problems raised in her novels. The political conflict between the two chief ministers is averted; Saroj finds Vishal; Jit and Mara get back together; finally, when everything seems to have broken down, Vishal's typist, Man Singh, does show up to type his memo to the Home Minister. The reconciliation and breakthrough evident in this work are not surpassed in the later fiction. Yes, the subject shifts and with it the quality of realization too, but its basic ingredients are already available in *Storm in Chandigarh*. This novel celebrates the triumph of Saroj's spirit under every kind of adversity, and thus the victory of good over evil, the human over the *asuric* and so on.

As to thematic shifts, I see them in two places in Sahgal's career. There is a shift after the first novel from the description of the social milieu in a small town to the problems of the beleaguered wife in *This Time of Morning*. The middle phase consists of five novels—*This Time of Morning, Storm in Chandigarh, The Day in Shadow, A Situation in New Delhi* and *Rich Like Us*—all of which have the women's question at their centre. With *Rich Like Us,* this problem seems to have been fully worked out, after which there is again a shift in subject in *Plans for Departure* and *Mistaken Identity*. Though *Plans for Departure* has a woman protagonist, she is not fighting the system as in the earlier novels. *Mistaken Identity* is entirely centred on a male protagonist, reminding us of *This Time of Morning*, the first novel.

The reasons for considering *Rich Like Us* a more mature and politically radical book are discussed very persuasively in Pankaj K. Singh's essay, "Feminism and Nayantara Sahgal's *The Day in Shadow* and *Rich Like Us*: From the Particular to the Ideological."[2] Singh argues that Sahgal has been moving to a recognizable feminist position, from the subjective point of view in *The Day in Shadow* to the objective evaluation of social conditions in *Rich Like Us:* "Unlike *The Day in Shadow* which almost naturalizes the arbitrary power dimension between the genders, *Rich Like Us* firmly rejects the arbitrary distribution of power, be it on the purely political level as it was during the Emergency or on the interpersonal and familial level as in the gender roles in society." (145) Singh substantiates her point by analyzing *The Day in Shadow* in detail. She sees a "central paradox" in "Simrit's overdependence on Raj": "In a novel that seemed to begin with a woman's decision to seek freedom, ironically it is man [sic] who constantly provides the norm." (140) She rightly points out that Simrit "passes on from one man's world into another man's" and that she "fails to see Raj's prejudices, biases, superficialities." (139-40) The book, in fact, ends with Raj's one-sided announcement of marriage before Ram Krishen.

Though Singh's article is full of insight, she tries to fit Sahgal into a feminist strait-jacket whereas the novelist would appear to reject the hegemony of any master-discourse. Indeed, Simrit's and Sahgal's feminism is imperfect. But it isn't very certain that Simrit sets out to be a feminist in the first place. Her decision to leave Som is not so much the assertion of equality or her quest for freedom as an act of survival. She is not a rebel to begin with. Moreover, Simrit has no quarrel with men or even with the apparent domination of men; what she rejects is a certain kind of man who embodies certain kind of values. Under the circumstances Raj comes across as a miraculous example of the male sex, so different from the other shallow and oppressive men in her life. Yes, Simrit is blind to Raj's own limitations as both a man and as a human being, but this if at all, is a drawback in her character, not in her ideological make-up as a feminist.

But the point that *Rich Like Us* is the more complex novel is well taken. Its narrative technique, for instance, is polyphonic. The book alternates between a limited third person narration and Sonali's first person narrative. The third person narrative is largely from the viewpoint of Rose, except for Chapters One, Six, Fifteen, Seventeen, and Twenty. The following summary may help to explain the structure of the novel:

Chapters	Point of View
One	Objective (moves from Neuman to Nishi, to Rose)
Two	Sonali
Three	Rose
Four	Sonali
Five	Rose
Six	Nishi
Seven	Sonali
Eight	Rose
Nine	Sonali
Ten	Rose
Eleven	Sonali
Twelve	Rose
Thirteen	Sonali
Fourteen	Rose
Fifteen	Kishori Lal
Sixteen	Rose
Seventeen	Kishori Lal
Eighteen	Rose
Nineteen	Sonali
Twenty	Nishi
Twenty-one	Sonali

Out of the twenty one chapters, Rose and Sonali have eight each, Nishi and Kishori Lal two each; the opening chapter is from a broader, though not omniscient point of view.

The Rose chapters tell the story of the Indo-British encounter, the gradual degeneration of modern Indian culture, and of Rose's life with Ram. The Sonali chapters are used to comment on the Emergency, to tell Ravi and Sonali's story, and also to trace the history of four generations of the Indian elite starting with Keshav Ranade's grandfather and coming to Sonali. The Nishi and Kishori Lal sections deal with the compromise of the new generation and the regeneration of the old.

To use Sonali's words in the beginning of the book, any reader of *Rich Like Us* soon becomes "obsessed with symbols." (31) We can use Roman Jacobson's famous categories of the metonymic versus metaphoric narrative modes to express this point. The novel operates simultaneously on essentially two levels, the literal and the figurative, the syntagmatic and the paradigmatic, the metonymic and the metaphoric, the synchronic and the diachronic. The first set refers to the narrative on the literal level which works on the basis of contiguity and succession. The second set refers to the figurative implications of the narrative, to its allegorical and metaphoric meaning, which work through substitution.[3]

At the literal level, *Rich Like Us* is the story of the Emergency as seen from the viewpoint of two main characters, Rose and Sonali. It is a compelling story even as it is. But it is on the metaphoric level that it assumes a stunning complexity and multi-valency. Indeed, seen from this perspective, the novel is a sustained allegory of modern India, especially of its relationship with Britain. What I offer below is a preliminary interpretation of the symbolic meaning of the major characters.

Character	*Description*	*Interpretation*
1. Rose	British, working class; in love with Ram; frank, clear-headed, compassionate, attractive.	The "good" West: liberal values, fair play, honesty; British empiricism, common-sense; anti-romantic, against superstition; the England that loved India, fought against Hitler, etc.

Rose is that part of Britain which crossed over to India and became a part of our past. True, her love for India and Ram may be a bit of a mystery; why she puts up with so much abuse from Ram is also not clear. But, Rose represents that aspect of Britain which loved India and was willing to suffer for it. Her working class origins distinguish her from her Imperialistic brethren. The name "Rose" itself suggests the mystic core of goodness within the West. Rose's candour, lack of self-deception, compassion, charity, empiricism, common-sense, and sense of fairplay are what Indian culture might benefit from.

2. Marcella	Crafted in terms of the "classic," upper class English beauty; sophisticated and ageless; also in love with India; marries into the British aristocracy.	Represents the ruling classes and their ambivalent attitude to India; Ram's affair with her symbolizes the "selling out" of Indian interests by our elites.

Marcella begins by being clearly aligned with Imperialism; her interest in things Indian is a sort of "orientalism." Her affair with Ram suggests that the Indian ruling classes will finally realign themselves with British ruling classes. Interestingly, she changes in the end by helping out Sonali. Almost like the British upper classes turning collaborators of India after independence and bailing out modern India (Sonali) from the clutches of fascism.

3. Ram	Indian, upper class; dapper; male chauvinist; bigamist; fascinated by British women; sensitive, intellectual, connoisseur of beauty; comatose at the beginning of the book.	The moribund aristocracy; morally corrupt; duplicitous, hypocritical, oppressors of women, yet charming, attractive; the "bad" aspects of Indian tradition somehow alluring; but, finally, helpless, confused, dying.

Ram is Hinduism or India trapped between the past and the present, tradition and modernity, India and the West. He is aligned both to traditional India (Mona) and Western modernity (Rose). But he is devoid of life-sustaining values. Ram is perhaps Hinduism or Indian tradition at its worst. In a sense, he is the real villain of the novel, not Dev. It is he who gives birth to Dev and does nothing to check the latter's misdemeanours. Dev's forging cheques in Ram's name refers to the misuse of tradition by modern politicians. Ram also represents patriarchal values; he is selfish, two-timing, and naive, but oppressive and insensitive nonetheless. Ram also shows the helplessness, the spineless confusion, and inertia of the Indian elite.

4. Ram's Father	The old Lalaji; anti-British; shrewd businessman; accepts Rose; honest and upright; the "real" entrepreneur.	Lalaji represents the "good," uncompromising, older generation; the real Indian tradition in a sense; he accepts Rose, which means he is not totally inflexible.

Rose and Lalaji together build up the fortunes of the family after partition. This means that the new Indian state is built upon the foundations of the "real" Indian tradition and modernity learned from the British.

5. Mona	Ram's first wife; traditional, pious, devoted; opposed to Rose at first, but makes up with her; spoils Dev.	Mona represents Indian womanhood; her devotion to Ram is monastic; she is the traditional woman, a loser and a sufferer; backward, but not "bad"; a victim; the doting mother who spoils Dev.

Mona is the traditional Indian woman—a giver, a loser, and a victim. She is never treated as an equal by Ram and scarcely as a human being, but she puts up with his abuse without a whimper. She is loyal, devoted, and stubborn. Religious, irrational, and superstitious, but not wicked or malicious. When Rose saves her life, she forgets the past and becomes her friend. Modernity thus, must save tradition; when the victim is saved, she accepts modernity. The typical Indian mother, Mona spoils her male offspring by not deconditioning him of the evils of his inheritance.

6. Sonali	Upper middle class, civil service background; daughter of an honest ICS officer; inherits the Gandhian legacy from her father but also liberalism from the West at Oxford; upright, though marginalized; the real India and the heroine of the book; survives in the end.	The "good" India; has got the best of both tradition and modernity; heterodox Hindu and Westernized liberal; critic of the emergency; independent working woman; strong, courageous; the culmination of the earlier Sahgal women; liberated but not necessarily feminist.

Sonali is the most important character in the novel. She represents the "good" India and also modern Indian womanhood. She combines the best of Indian tradition and modernity. She is aware of the evil in traditional Hinduism because of the *sati* of her great-grandmother; she is the new virtuous woman for whom virtue is courage, not self-sacrifice. She is aligned with Rose and with the anti-emergency forces. Her remaining single points to the deficiency in modern Indian manhood. Ravi's failure to measure up to her is the failure of Indian men in general. Therefore, she is forced to remain single. Yet, she is neither helpless nor unhappy. She is marginalized, treated unfairly by the system, but she does not lose heart. Her survival in the end is a sign of hope for modern India.

7. Keshav Ranade	ICS; bureaucrat; withers away after the Emergency is declared on 26 June, 1975.	Bureaucrat of the old school; kind, upright, reformist Hindu; not a part of the Kashmiri "mafia."

Ranade seems to be modelled on Sahgal's own father, Ranjit Pandit. He represents the old bureaucracy which was nourished by the freedom movement. He has also inherited from his father the legacy of his grandmother's *sati*. This makes him critical of tradition. Sonali is closely aligned to him, certainly his heir emotionally and spiritually.

8. Ravi Kachru	IAS; Oxford educated bureaucrat; supports the Emergency; replaces Sonali; changes in the end.	The "new" bureaucrat; guided not by norms but by expediency; essentially spineless; prefers readymade and easy answers to hard facts and analysis; also a victim in the end.

Ravi has been Sonali's lover at Oxford, but has somehow turned back on his essence. He exemplifies compromise; the pliant bureaucrat, he actually plays a key role in the success of the Emergency. He lacks both courage and convictions. Allows himself to be used by the politicians. Thinks he is in control when he is actually a puppet. Shows a superficial assimilation of the West and an inadequate understanding of India. He belongs to a very old type in Indian politics, the courtier. Ultimately a case of self-delusion and self-betrayal. Meant to contrast the bureaucrat of the old school, Ranade.

9. Dev	Rich, spoiled, brat; stupid and selfish; cruel, materialistic, opportunistic; becomes a new entrepreneur and finally a minister; Rose's killer.	A Sanjay Gandhi like figure; a monster who represents Emergency; the worst of both tradition and modernity; the lumpen element in Indian politics.

Dev is the child of the worst aspects of Indian tradition. He represents violence, greed, selfishness, cruelty—in a word, Indian politics gone bad. His stupidity and amnesia indicate that the new breed of politicians have no knowledge of their past. They have learned nothing from the Indian freedom movement. They are fascistic and violent. His killing of Rose suggests not only that he is utterly immoral, but that he has no use for the lessons of liberalism, democracy or modernity.

10. Nishi	Lower middle-class girl who marries rich; another victim who accepts the lies of the emergency for personal benefit, but is betrayed by it, in her father's arrest.	Represents the survival instinct without a corresponding value-system; shares the failure of Dev's generation in forgetting the past; ultimately, also a victim more than an oppressor.

Nishi is a child of the partition. Growing up in a lower middle class home, she first tries to secure her future. She refuses to see that in her quest for affluence she is violating most of the laws of the country. Similarly, she refuses to see the evil that is in Dev. She and her socialite friends represent the failure of the elite to safeguard the interests of the country. Their active collaboration with the Emergency is motivated by self-interest and greed; this shows not just the apathy of the ruling classes but their willingness to sell the country for their own gains.

11. Kishori Lal	Another old timer like Ram's father; failed academic; post-partition, small-time trader; but still retains ambitions of doing good; stubborn and headstrong; his character really blossoms in jail, when he's tortured.	Exemplifies the breakdown of civil rights during the emergency; victim of police brutality and torture; uses techniques of *satyagraha* in jail; again, shows the hidden strengths of the middle class.

Kishori Lal is an ordinary middle class person, a petty trader. His life is already a failure; the partition has defeated him. His arbitrary arrest shows the complete breakdown of law and order during the Emergency. This event, however, actually brings out the best in him. He learns to resist injustice and tyranny like a *satyagrahi*. His befriending the tortured student is an instance of heroism lurking within the middle class.

12. The crippled beggar	Landlords have broken his hands and legs; he lies by the tomb, passive, but not unintelligent; knows who killed Rose; may get a pair of artificial limbs by the end of the book.	The beggar represents the Indian masses who have been battered and crippled by the ruling classes. They are silent and helpless, but not yet dead. They are victims of endless oppression and injustice.

The crippled beggar is perhaps the most important symbol in the book. His arms and legs have been broken by the landlord whom he was trying to oppose. This shows the suppression of the Indian masses by the brute force of the ruling classes. Rose is the only one who befriends him, who treats him like a human being. It is only a Western sense of the autonomy of the individual and the respect for the dignity of each human being which will enable us to see the downtrodden people of India as our equals. Everyone else only thinks of him as an eyesore, the typical attitude of the elite to the suffering masses. The elites have failed in their obligations to the underprivileged. Only Rose's attempts to give him a pair of artificial arms might help restore his dignity and usefulness as a human being. He sees Rose's murder but is helpless. The masses, likewise, witness the atrocities, oppressions, and injustices that surround them but are powerless to resist.

Putting all these interpretations together, we see that *Rich Like Us*, though a bleak book, does not despair totally. Sonali survives and there is a hint at the end that the Emergency will end after all. The crippled beggar, too, may get his hands back. Also, Kachru becomes Ravi again, disillusioned by the excesses of the Emergency. So there is hope for the bureaucracy too. Overall, in *Rich Like Us* it does appear that India will survive—but just about.

In spite of this guarded optimism, it is Sahgal's most gloomy book. The murder of Rose is the nadir of Sahgal's pessimism. Never before or after has a main character been murdered so tragically and helplessly. There is also a real *sati* in this book, not just reports of rape, burning and torture. We see the brutality of the police, the politicians, and the landlords. Peasant women are raped and fed into brick kilns; their husbands are beaten or maimed when they try to resist oppression. We see the lumpenization of Indian politics and the abuse of power on an unprecedented scale.

But while the book is very self-critical, it is soft on the West. Everything about the West is seen favourably. Even imperialism, so obviously the enemy during the freedom movement, doesn't have strong critics in the book. Ranade is merely an agonized and confused spectator of the last days of the Raj. The book, thus, lacks a strong anti-Western centre. While India is viewed critically throughout, the West is seen as if with tinted glasses.[4]

Rose, Marcella, and even Freddie or Minnie are positive characters. While blaming ourselves and our traditions, Sahgal would appear to condone the violence of colonialism and capitalism. She sees the West as the repository of not just liberal values, but of human rights, decency, democracy, and civil liberties. India, by contrast, becomes a dark continent, dominated by disease, poverty, injustice, oppression, religious superstition, communalism, casteism, bigamy, *sati*, rape, torture, violation of civil rights, corrupt politicians and bureaucrats, greedy and callous socialites, exploitative ruling classes, crushed and defeated masses, and so on.

This, according to me, is a drawback. It also makes the motivation for Rose's character weak. What exactly is it that attracts her and makes her hold on to Ram? Why does she put up with so much rubbish from him? This isn't clear. It would seem that Rose is mesmerized by Ram and India, tied by mysterious threads of destiny to both. The narrator tells us that after meeting Ram, she had "entered an emotional labyrinth and she was drawn magnetically on . . . a victim of casual unthinking sorcery." Many years later, she tells Freddie: "You know how it was with me, Freddie, when I came out here. It wasn't me making up my mind. It was outside me, bigger. If I was a Hindu and believed in other lives, I'd say I must've been here before and wanted to come back." (107)[5]

Sahgal appears to be falling back on those old stereotypes of the labyrinthian, complex, and mysterious mind of the Hindu versus the simple, straightforward, commonsensical Westerner. Surely, this is a mystification. The English came to India for profit; later they colonized us for profit. Moreover, in the novel, Ram isn't even complex in any attractive or superior way. His polish is merely superficial, a gloss or veneer which peels off on closer observation. Rose's motivations, then, are too vague to be convincing.

The only way to solve the mystery that is Rose is to consider her as someone who has learned from India, not one who comes to teach us. She belongs to the Mrs. Moore type of Englishwoman who has a mysterious love for India, a spiritual affinity with our culture. This semi-mystic type doesn't quite fit Rose, as we know. Likewise, it would be hard to make a case for Rose's representing the best of Indian traditions because she never quite loses her Englishness. She not only retains her cockney accent till the end, but her room, a small English preserve in an otherwise Indian household, is a marker of her identity, her attempt to preserve a continuity with her English past. A more charitable way for regarding her would be to see her as an adventurer, someone who crosses boundaries, whose zest for life is their motivating force. But, again, why would an adventurer stay on through the kind of travail that Rose endures, only to be murdered in the end?

Rose is not the only problem with the book. The depiction of the entire Indo-British encounter is, ultimately, unsatisfactory. This is an important issue because the book itself is dedicated to "The Indo-British Experience and what its sharers have learned from each other." If this is indeed the key theme of the book, then it turns out that they have, indeed, very little to learn from us and while we have a lot to learn from them. This inequality in Sahgal's portrayal of the encounter is disappointing. While it is true that Sahgal would have us accept all those who came to us from the West and gave us, so to speak, their lives without dividing them into the "good" and the "bad," while she would have us own up to the totality of our mixed inheritance, she still fails to offer any lessons to our "Other," the West. What have they got from us? If we were to believe Sahgal's account in *Rich Like Us,* then it would be bigamy, hypocrisy, intolerance, and finally a cruel death.

No wonder, because Ram or Dev are the worst possible representatives of India that Sahgal could have thought of. Ram's charm is superficial; actually, he is a self-centred and wilful liar. He lacks both integrity and character. He is a shallow person, with little knowledge of either India or Europe. Quite inferior to Vishal, Raj or Shivraj, he is a poor representative of India. And Dev, his idiotic, frighteningly amoral, and murderous son, a pathological case of a diseased Indian mind, is an even worse example of an India.

On the other hand, British characters are, invariably, portrayed at their best. Even Marcella, superficial, upper class, predatory, redeems herself in the end by extending a helping hand to Sonali. Does this mean that the British aristocracy will always retain their values while the Indian elites betray them? And must Sonali, the modern Indian woman if not modern India herself, live on the handouts of the West when the novel ends? Even in Sonali's grandfather's manuscript, Mr. Timmons, the collector, comes out a real hero, a liberal, paternalistic *sahib*. His friendship with Keshav's grandfather is unconvincing; the turn of the century was the period when the sense of empire was, perhaps, the strongest. The divide between the ruled and the ruler, black and white, Indian and English, was then at its height. How implausible to suggest that Keshav's father recuperated at the Timmons as he recovered the shock of his mother's *sati*. If Mr. Timmons was all that great, why didn't his assistants prevent the illegal self-immolation? Not just Rose, Marcella, or Mr. Timmons emerge angelic in Sahgal's novel, the minor British characters are also real "good guys." Rose's parents, limited but brave, working class people, who in their own way stand up to Hitler, and die in the blitz. Freddie, good old Freddie: such a nice loser in love, the typical British sport; brave Freddie who fights for his country and the rest of the free world against Hitler's hellish hordes. Minnie, part of the lower order of the British in India, is so cultured and polite to Rose nonetheless. If the Indo-British encounter were to be judged from this book it would appear that the British are the ones who are civilized, while we are the barbarians. Isn't this the image which colonialism sought to propagate? Remember the white man's burden and the civilizing mission of Empire? Isn't Sahgal, in her moments of despair with the Indian scene, unwittingly reproducing such colonialist stereotypes?

There are other flaws in the novel, the chief of which is the *sati* incident. That a *sati* could happen in a family so progressive and advanced is perhaps Sahgal's deliberate note of warning, if not the representation of an actual event. But the manner of its portrayal is still unconvincing. Ranade's grandmother doesn't seem to be the sort to be pushed around easily, let alone murdered. The motivation for her consent isn't worked out sufficiently: it seems that she agreed to commit *sati* as a part of a deal with her brother-in-law about her son's inheritance. (135) But this aspect isn't brought out clearly or emphasized. The self-sacrifice or strength of character of Ranade's grandmother are, similarly, not demonstrated in her sudden self-immolation. The whole effect is painful and confused, almost as if the event were too horrible, too unbearable to even fictionalize. Also, a *sati* after the cremation of the husband is technically impossible unless the widow was not available during the cremation (not true in this case) or if she were menstruating (not indicated in this case). So the whole incident seems somewhat lurid and hazy, however powerful in symbolic import.[6]

The chronology of the novel has been meticulously planned from the time of Sonali's great-grandfather. Similarly, Rose's story too has an elaborate chronology, going back to her birth in 1912. But at least at one point the scheme seems to fail. We are told that in August 1969 Ranade is fifty two. (150) This means that he was born in 1917. We know that Sonali was born in 1937 (she is thirty eight in 1975). This means that Ranade was twenty when his daughter was born. We know that Sonali is the younger daughter (160); so Kiran has to be born before 1937. Wouldn't that make Ranade an implausibly young father?[7]

In conclusion, it seems to me that *Rich Like Us* is an important, ambitious, but flawed book. While its depiction of the Indo-British encounter is unsatisfactory, its handling of the problem of women is both insightful and socially relevant. Rose and Sonali embody two different versions of the story of the oppression of contemporary women. Rose doesn't give up, but is killed; Sonali, who also fights back against the system, survives. Is Sahgal suggesting that only through inner strength, self-reliance, independence even unto spinsterhood, can women live with dignity and self-respect in India?

NOTES

1. *Nayantara Sahgal* (New Delhi: Arnold Heinemann, 1978), pp. 45-67.
2. In *Feminism and Recent Fiction in English*, ed. Sushila Singh (New Delhi: Prestige, 1991), pp. 147-53.
3. See Roman Jacobson on the Metaphoric and Metonymic poles in his essay, "Two Aspects of Language and Two Types of Linguistic Disturbances," in R. Jacobson and M. Halle, *Fundamentals of Language* (The Hague: Mouton, 1956). Also see David Lodge's *The Modes of Writing.* (London: Routledge, 1977).

   Frederic Jameson's argument that Third World texts are often political allegories (*Social Text*, 15, Fall 1986) is particularly apt in this context. However, to the best of my knowledge, mine is the first essay that attempts such a reading of *Rich Like Us.* The commonplace view of the novel, on the other hand, comes from reading it literally only as a political novel that indicts the Emergency. See Jasbir Jain, "The Emperor's New Clothes: The Emergency and Sahgal's *Rich Like Us*," *The New Indian Novel in English,* ed. Viney Kirpal (Delhi: Allied, 1990), pp. 27-35, and O.P. Mathur, "The Nausea of Totalitarianism: A Note on Nayantara Sahgal's *Rich Like Us*," *World Literature Today,* 65.1 (Winter 1991), pp. 68-71 as examples.

4. Uma Parameswaran makes the following observation in her critical review of *Rich Like Us* in *World Literature Today,* 60.2 (Spring 1986): "One would think that the misguided stereotyping of the English as the cream of human intelligence, the milk of human kindness, the backbone of human fortitudes, would have been buried with colonial imperialism." (pp. 361-62) Despite the clumsiness and the mixed metaphors, Parameswaran's comment seems justified.
5. Nayantara Sahgal, *Rich Like Us* (London: Heinemann, 1985).
6. In a letter to this writer dated 26 August 1991, Ms. Sahgal acknowledged the *sati* in the book was based on an incident in her own family. Her paternal great-grandmother (Ranjit Pandit's grandmother) committed *sati.* But I am concerned with the fictional representation of this event within *Rich Like Us* and its appropriateness to its immediate context.

   I would like to express my deepest gratitude to Ms. Sahgal for being so generous and kind as to read a draft of this paper and to offer numerous, valuable suggestions on how it might be improved.
7. May I be permitted to a small aside on the name, "Ranade"? Keshav Ranade is described as a Saraswat brahmin in *Rich Like Us*, but Ranade is a surname which only Chitpavan (or Konkanastha) Brahmins have. Perhaps, Sahgal ought to have chosen a different name.

Feminism vis-a-vis Woman's Dignity: A Study of Shashi Deshpande's *That Long Silence*

T. ASOKA RANI

Feminism has come to mean a movement in support of the principle that women should have the same rights and opportunities, e.g. legal, political, social, economic etc., as men. A reference to it in the treatise *Half the Sky* reads as "By feminism we mean both the awareness of women's position in society as one of disadvantage or inequality compared with that of men and also a desire to remove those disadvantages."[1] Feminists try to identify the deeprooted causes leading to oppression of women and endeavour to remove, as far as possible, such causes. They try to bring about a change in the social milieu wherein women are accepted as equals, in all respects, to men in the equitable sharing of rights, opportunities and also responsibilities in the process of evolution of human society. Some restrict their demands to equality in matters relating to education and work with an eye on economic self-reliance. There are others among the feminists who call for a drastic change of the entire panorama of social fabric with a view to doing away lock, stock and barrel with the tradition-bound, entrenched belief in the moral superiority of man over woman. Their cry is to eradicate the persisting gender-discrimination in all its manifestations.

Feminism is often defined as a struggle against all forms of patriarchal and sexiest oppression. The moment such oppression is eliminated, feminism *ipso facto* ceases to exist: "the aim of feminism as an emancipatory theory becomes to abolish itself along with its opponent."[2] But such a consummation is a far cry, given the existing status of women in the contemporary Indian society. Intensification of feminist activity seems to be the only way towards panacea for the ills in the society militating against women.

Down the ages, the place of women in the tradition-bound, male-dominated Indian society had been very unenviable. Women were treated as no more than mere chattels; they were confined to the four walls of the house. Freedom enjoyed by men in different fields of activity was considered a male prerogative and, therefore, denied to women. The seeds of emancipation of women were sown by the British rulers, thanks to their sagacity and foresight, by their patronage and encouragement of women's education. Leaders and reformers like Raja Rammohan Roy, Bal Gangadhar Tilak, Mahatma Gandhi and a host of other luminaries rendered yeoman service for the upliftment of women. Even after Independence, the position of women—economic, social and cultural—in almost every stratum of Indian society remains far from reassuring. A vast majority of women in families outside the pale of civilized society are reconciled to a life of humiliation in the form of gender-bias while performing the roles of wives and mothers in the rigidly custom-bound milieu they live in. But what is shockingly true is that even women with liberal modern education, with an irrepressible yearning to break loose from the time-honoured crippling and iniquitous social laws condemning women to a role subordinate to that of men, do often lose their moorings and find themselves in perilously embarrassing situations due to a variety of reasons. There are instances galore where working women with sound economic potential are also not able to steer clear of the besetting pitfalls created by the customs and beliefs sedulously preserved in the tradition-bound Indian society.

Slowly becoming aware of the injustice heaped on them, women began to raise their voice in protest and this led to the birth of women's liberation movement in the early 70s. Elite women confined to major cities were initially drawn into the vortex of these feminist movements and their primary role was to bring home to the women in the diverse sections of society how they were subjected to iniquitous and humiliating treatment in this custom-bound, male-dominated environment.

With the passage of time, more and more votaries of feminism joined the ranks of the movement. Kali for Women, a feminist publishing house has come into being and it is publishing books on women by women. The feminist journal *Manushi* is focussing on the women's problems. Besides such crusading efforts by the media, several fora are interacting with women even in the rural areas to awaken them to the age-old pestering canker of sex-bias afflicting the society.

The position of women in the society is slowly but steadily changing for the better, following their unremitting assertion of their individuality by turning their wrath against the humiliating conventions assiduously nurtured by man down the ages. Women are beginning to take part in the affairs of the world, but one must not close one's eyes to the fact that, after all, it is still a world that belongs to man. They have yet to traverse a long way towards their goal of taking up their position alongside men on terms of perfect equality. As long as the gender discrimination, in whatever measure, continues, the clash of male-female identity is also bound to be there. And as long as this clash persists, deleterious consequences such as the breakdown of marriages and, worse still, women taking recourse to horrendous forms of suicide continue to plague our society. This problem, which is defying a solution despite several decades of reformist efforts, statutory and otherwise, affects the self-respect of women constituting half of the human race.

It is said that literature of any country is the store-house of information on the cultural and sociological aspects of its people. "The role of the writer is to feel the pulse of the society, know its sickness and suggest such cures as are in consonance with its culture."[3] Feminists argue that literature all along has been tuned to the point of view of the male element. Woman is often "marginalized," "repressed" or "silenced" in literary works. An idealized image of woman is presented in literature concealing the bitter reality of her position in patriarchal society. Alice Jardine attempts to define feminism as a "movement from the point of view of, by, and for women."[4] It is therefore imperative that women writers write from women's point of view, write boldly about their own emotions and experiences. Bringing about the difference in male and female experience and its expression in literature, Virginia Woolf says that "there is the obvious and enormous difference of experience in the first place; but the essential difference lies in the fact not that men describe battles and women the birth of children, but that each sex describes itself."[5] She also desired that she should write and be read only as a woman and not as a 'surrogate' for man. The women writers therefore have to write constructively to provide role models for the oppressed women. By reinterpreting old myths and questioning the validity of traditions and customs that circumscribe women in narrow slots, Indian women novelists have to continue challenging the operating codes of morality which subordinate women in the social structure.

The emergence of women novelists has considerably influenced Indian life and society. The depiction of women reflects a shift in the sensibility of the writer as well as the reader. Shashi Deshpande, comparatively a recent entrant into the literary scene, portrays the new Indian woman and her dilemma in her novels. She concerns herself with the plight of the modern Indian woman trying to understand herself and to preserve her identity as wife, mother and above all as a human being.

Feminists are primarily concerned with the recognition of woman as a being, an autonomous being. They want woman to realize herself through self-analysis. Such a quest for one's own identity forms the theme of Shashi Deshpande's novel, *That Long Silence*. Jaya, the protagonist thinks of her past days and tries to analyze herself, "to decide who she really is."[6]

The fact that Jaya was rechristened as Suhasini by her husband on their wedding day confuses Jaya in her search for an identity. The pseudonym under which she operates as a writer further complicates the issue. Jaya stands for revolt whereas Suhasini symbolizes submission. Jaya rejects the name Suhasini and it is significant as a manifestation of her protest against such customs. But her sense of identity is never certain. She is torn between being Jaya, herself and Suhasini, the good wife; between building a self as a writer and a self as a wife and mother. Through the process of reliving the past in her mind, Jaya gets the guidance for her future. She decides to break her long seventeen years of silence and gives up being a passive and silent partner to Mohan. She decides to assert herself as an individual and also as a woman, wife or mother. Though she chooses to remain in the family, a change has been wrought in her situation. She has come out of the confining slots allotted to her by the patriarchal society. Earlier, Jaya had denied certain parts of herself that did not fit into the strait jacket of wifehood. Now she asserts: "I am not afraid any more. The panic has gone. I'm Mohan's wife, I had thought, and cut off the bits of me that had refused to be Mohan's wife. Now I know that kind of a fragmentation is not possible. The child, hands in pockets, has been with me through the years. She is with me still." (191)[7] Sarla Palkar calls this novel a 'feminist critique' because of bald statements like this. If exposing patriarchal practices is the principal objective of feminist criticism, "this is what Shashi Deshpande also does through her text."[8]

Inspired by the feminist movements in the West, some Indian women, in their eagerness for freedom, made a total switch over to the other side, seeking freedom from everything, including from their culture. Shashi Deshpande's protagonists find freedom not in the western sense but in conformity with the society they live in without drifting away from one's culture. Jaya's decision is not a meek surrender to circumstances, but a sensible compromise between the mutually conflicting ideals of conformity and non-conformity.

Shashi Deshpande does not take kindly to the theory that 'women are victims.' The 'dependency syndrome' in women is responsible for their victimization and she desires that women need to offer resistance and emerge as strong-willed individuals to face life, to share responsibilities and not to escape from it.

Feminism in its early stages visualized an exclusively all-female world where men would have only peripheral functions. However, the present day feminist thought, while seeking to destroy masculinist hierarchy, is not against sexual dualism. Feminism is necessarily pro-woman but it need not be anti-man. Affirming such a view, P.

Ramamoorthi aptly remarks: "The attempts to create 'female enclaves' are extremist reactions but the recent trends in feminist literature are an indication that it is possible for a woman to live in the world where men also live."[9]

Shashi Deshpande too appears to hold a similar view, rejecting a separatist stance. Aware of the fact that breaking off the bonds of family would result in loneliness and disintegration of the larger social set-up, Jaya looks for happiness and self-fulfilment within the family itself. She asks for her individuality to be valued equally along with that of man. As long as one half of the humanity is denied decent and dignified life, it will be a far cry to hope for a better world. But, Jaya, confident of her individuality and hopeful of a change in Mohan's attitude, moves beyond the cultural stereotypes with the firm conviction that 'life has always to be made possible.' Such an optimistic ending of the novel, *That Long Silence* shows that the day is not far off when men and women are valued equally, ensuring unsullied dignity, individuality and self-respect to women.

NOTES

1. The Bristol Women's Studies Group, ed., *Half the Sky: An Introduction to Women's Studies* (London: Virago, 1979), p. 3.
2. Sushila Singh, "Recent Trends in Feminist Thought: *A Tour de Horizon*," *Indian Women Novelists*, ed. R.K. Dhawan (New Delhi: Prestige, 1991), Set I, Vol. 1, p. 59.
3. Sita Ram Jaiswal, "The Role of the Writer Today," *The Indian P.E.N.* (July-August 1976), p. 14.
4. Alice Jardine, qtd. in Sushila Singh, p. 61.
5. Virginia Woolf, *Contemporary Writers* (London: Hogarth, 1965), p. 26.
6. Sarabjit Sandhu, "The Image of Woman in *That Long Silence*," *Indian Women Novelists,* Set I, Vol. V, p. 138.
7. Shashi Deshpande, *That Long Silence* (New Delhi: Penguin, 1989).
8. Sarla Palkar, "Breaking the Silence: *That Long Silence*," *Indian Women Novelists,* Set I, Vol. V, p. 169.
9. P. Ramamoorthi, "My Life is my own: A Study of Shashi Deshpande's Women," *Indian Women Novelists*, Set I, Vol. V, p. 38.

Dissonance and Harmony in Shashi Deshpande's *The Binding Vine*

RAMA NAIR

Shashi Deshpande's *The Binding Vine*[1] is prefaced by a notable quote from Emily Bronte's *Wuthering Heights*: 'What were the use of my creation if I were entirely contained here?' This, in effect, encapsulates the dilemma encountered by the urban woman of the nineties. The modern Indian woman is educated, intelligent, and aware. But the inequalities of the female sex that lie beneath this facade of independence and apparent self-confidence, belie her attempts at creating and sustaining a distinct identity of her own. An awareness of the ironies of the feminine condition is a recurrent theme of the fiction of the nineties. The Indian woman writer in English, while treating the basic problem of survival, found new ways to counter the various forms of oppression that was meted out to women in what is still, a male-dominated society. The female protagonists in these feminocentric novels are no revolutionaries. But in their attempt to survive, they successfully create a niche for themselves. They were more concerned with the minutiae of everyday existence. Their suffering was mental, emotional, and psychological. The contradictions that existed within one led to a divide within oneself. This divide was the one that was 'the hardest to bridge; the hardest to accept, to live with.'[1]

Shashi Deshpande's *The Binding Vine* is embedded in a specific context. The narrator is Urmila or Urmi who is clever, educated and sharp tongued. The narrative begins with Urmi grieving over the death of her one-year old daughter, Anu. She is deeply affected by her loss, and her despair is evident in her confession that 'this emptiness, this blankness frightens me.' (20) The 'smell of hopelessness haunts me now . . . I've lost hope entirely; I used it all up in that one day and night of frenzied hoping and there's nothing left.' (21) She isolates herself mentally from those closest to her. These include her husband, her mother, mother-in-law, and sister-in-law. But ironically enough, it is this alienation that leads her closer to life. The novel unfolds itself into a psychological description of a complex female character's final acceptance of life on its own terms.

In the narrative, the protagonist uses the story of her life to construct a plot where the different definitions of female life are recreated in a new form. This plot/story distinction is based on the framework developed by Viktor Shlovsky for analyzing narrative. He distinguished between the story (fabula), i.e., the 'raw temporal-causal sequence of narrated events, and the plot (*szujet*), i.e., the way in which these 'raw materials' are formally manipulated in unconventional ways that make the audience reconsider the usual ordering of events.[2]

The story is the conventional one—of a woman's biography, beginning with childhood, marriage and motherhood. The plot emerges from 'the unexpected twists in the narrative that draw attention to differences from the conventional story, thus defamiliarizing the taken-for-granted assumptions.'[3] The tension that arises between the plot and the expected story is indicated through various narrative devices. The plot reframes experiences which were formally felt to be dissonant with social expectations by constituting them as new cultural possibilities.'

Motherhood is the dominant motif in the narrative discourse. The stories of pregnancy, birth and mothering are not related as ordinary events in the life of a woman. They are retold as significant experiences which have the capacity to destroy, nurture or reactivate the destiny of a woman. The narrative fabric of *The Binding Vine* is interwoven with the experiences of three mothers—Urmi, Mira and Shakutai. These events take on new meaning as the narrator realigns her self in relation to these diverse experiences. Out of dissonance, a pattern of reintegration follows.

Urmi is married to Kishore, a man whom she had once loved. Kishore was in the Merchant Navy, and so away for long stretches of time. Earlier in their marriage, Kishore had appeared unemotional and withdrawn to Urmi. He was neither spontaneous nor emotional like her. But after the death of their baby, Anu, Kishore had become absolutely uncommunicative. As Urmi states, 'Yes, here it is, the knowledge, I spared myself then. Kishore will never remove his armour, there is something in him I will never reach. I have lived with the hope that some day I will.' (141) The death of Anu acts as a catalyst, and Urmi is compelled to re-define her relationship with Kishore.

Mira was Urmi's dead mother-in-law. She had died while giving birth to Kishore, and Kishore's father had married again. Mira had been married at eighteen. Mira's story was revealed through her brief entries in her diary. These entries provide a glimpse into a life lived painfully and secretively. 'Cloistered in a home, living with a man she could not love, surrounded by people she had nothing in common with—how did she go on?' (127) But, Urmi reflected, maybe it was her writing that kept her going, kept her alive. Through Mira's letters and poems (undisclosed and unpublished), Urmi discovered an unhappy woman who questioned silently the relevance of her 'traditional' role of wife and mother. In one of her letters, written after her mother was dead, and when she found herself with child again Mira had written: 'My mother is dead. She died happy, they tell me. She saw me married, she saw me pregnant, and she was happy. . . . But I can find no comfort in it, not for myself, anyway. . . . She knew I was not happy, I knew she knew it; but she was afraid to ask me, afraid I would admit it.' (126) The finality of despair, echoing a fear that one can never escape, is there in her poem,

> Whose face is this I see in the mirror,
> Unsmiling, grave, bedewed with fear?
> The daughter? No, Mother, I am now your shadow. (126)

But impending motherhood brought with it, involuntarily, a desire to live. In her poem about her unborn child she wrote,

> Lightning flashed through the front door
> and I who was stone quivered,
> Bridging two worlds, you awaken in me a desire for life. (136-37)

But Desire, says the Buddha is the cause of grief.

> but how escape this cord this binding vine of love?
> Fear lies coiled within this womb-piercing joy. (136-37)

Mira wrote nothing after this poem. She died at 22, without ever seeing her new-born child.

The interpersonal context revealed through the interpolation of Mira's personal history in the main narrative structure indicates how Urmi's life shapes and evolves through this relationship. In feminist literature, "this reliance may well be a function of women's relative powerlessness, their lack of access to more formal and institutional routes to influence and as such a survival strategy."[4] Urmi's experiences acquire meaning when assessed in the context of Mira's life-story.

The second female character whose life intersects Urmi's is Shakutai. Shakutai was an ordinary, lower middle-class woman. Her teenaged daughter, Kalpana, brutally raped and mutilated by an unknown person, had been hospitalized. It was in this hospital that Urmi met Shakutai, and Dr. Bhasker Jain. A relationship between unequals—as between Urmi and Shakutai—becomes a context for interpreting Urmi's own personal narrative. Kalpana's and Mira's life appear to bear similarities. Mira had been reduced to a stereotyped feminine role-model, while Kalpana was yet another aspect of the submissive and passive portrayal of womanhood. In a largely hostile patriarchal culture, one of the ways in which women were dominated was either through a forced marriage, or through sexually perverted acts outside marriage, as in rape.

Beneath the apparently conforming surface of the women's narratives, lie either techniques of evasion or concealment. Mira had evaded any open discussion of her tensions. Her diary had been her sole confidence. Kalpana's plight was interpreted as a shameful calamity which would have social repercussions on her whole family. So Kalpana's mother, initially, attempted concealment of the fact. The traumas of motherhood are heightened as Shakutai's love conflicts with her despairing resentment against her daughter. To her, it was not the fault of the man. 'The man,' she had said to Urmi, 'What use is it blaming him? . . . We have to keep to our places, we can never step out. I warned Kalpana, but she would never listen to one . . . that's why this happened to her . . . women must know fear.' (148)

But, as Urmi reasons out later, was it because Shakutai like all parents wanted to shake off the burden of guilt all parents bore? Her daughter's youth and beauty had made her vulnerable. Kalpana's joy in her existence had been interpreted by her mother as 'wayward.' So mothers unconsciously hoped for sons because they were frightened of bearing this constant burden of fear of their daughter as well.

Shakutai had wanted the best for her daughter. 'Sometimes Urmila,' she said, 'I was cruel to the girl; but I did it for her. I wanted her to have all that I never had—education, a good life, a good marriage, respect from others.' And again, 'I did not want her to be born, is that why she's dying now? Is this my punishment?' (112) Shakutai had sent Kalpana to her sister, Sulu, and her husband, Prakash, who were childless and who had promised to educate and look after Kalpana. But in spite of Sulu's devotion, the girl had run away from them in three days. Kalpana, in spite of beatings and scoldings had refused to go back. The narrative takes a dramatic turn with Sulu's suicide. Shakutai, who depended on Sulu, morally and emotionally, was shattered. But the truth was that it was Prakash, Kalpana's uncle, who had raped Kalpana when he realized that he could not marry her, and that she hated him and his advances. In Mira and in Kalpana, the mothers 'betray' their daughters. In wanting the 'best' for them, they paradoxically, invite only death and disaster for them.

The feminist theory which distinguishes between biological sex and socially constructed gender is evident here. The events are used to deconstruct the feminine role. The distinction between biological sex and socially constructed gender is foregrounded to give different examples of the construction of feminity. It raises Julia Kristeva's question, what is a woman? Does feminity reside in biology, gender attributes, or, as Kristeva suggests, in the marginal position assigned to the female sex in the dominant culture?[5]

In *The Binding Vine*, it would appear, the theme is not the construction of feminity, but its deconstruction. The psychological transformation that Urmi achieves is through the psychoanalytic approaches to gender rather than sociological ones. Deshpande takes the feminine point of view, and emphasizes the suffering and alienation which women as daughters and mothers endure. But the psychological transformation that Urmi achieves is more through an awareness and a realization of the multiple and contrary identities which a woman possesses. Urmi, herself, had to bind together her conflicting identities of 'neglected' daughter, 'abandoned' wife, and grieving mother.

Once Urmi was asked by her brother, Amrut, 'Do women want to be dominated?' Urmi's answer was that no human being wants to be dominated. Love was the most important need. 'From the moment of our birth,' Urmi tells him, 'we struggle to find something with which we can anchor ourselves to this strange world we find ourselves in. Only when we love do we find this anchor.' (137) But love makes one vulnerable. So we put on an 'armour,' and in the process of surviving we do terrible things. The main urge was always to survive. The answer to 'What shall I do?' in the face of life's interminable problems is silence. Sages and philosophers had tried to find an answer. But 'Detachment, love, brotherhood, non-violence—they're just words. They mean nothing to our living. Dharma, Dharma, Dharma, the *Mahabharata* endlessly, tirelessly repeats. Yet at the end, the poet cries out in despair, 'I raise my arms and I shout, but no one listens.' (202)

Though the utter futility of living overwhelms one, one is also terrified by the thought of dying, of ceasing to be. Mira had realized this. It is the 'binding vine' of love, with its cruelty and its selflessness, that binds together the conflicting multiple identities of one's self. Mira had found peace at the thought of the child within her. Shakutai discovered that she had to go on with the routine tasks of life for Kalpana and her other children, or stop living. Urmi's 'armour' falls away at her mother's belated confession that she loved her.

An integrated consciousness may be an illusion for ordinary mortals—but the 'spring of life' is refilled and nurtured through the redemptive powers of love. Love is compassion, and tolerance in dealing with the ordinary occurrences of everyday life. One can never opt out of this 'chakravyuha' of human existence. Love is the only factor that prevents us from falling apart. And this Urmi understands through a recollection of those instances that had embodied tenderness and affection. Through the lives of Mira and Shakutai, Urmi realizes that the identities she possesses transcend gender divisions. It is as an individual that her search for happiness begins.

NOTES

1. Shashi Deshpande, *The Binding Vine* (Delhi: Penguin, 1992), p. 201.
2. *Interpreting Women's Lives, Feminist Theory and Personal Narratives*, ed. Personal Narratives Group (Bloomington and Indianapolis: Indianapolis Univ. Press, 1989), p. 64.
3. *Ibid.*
4. *Ibid.*, p. 20.
5. Paulina Palmer, *Contemporary Women's Fiction, Narrative Practice and Feminist Theory* (Hertfordshire: Harvester Wheatsheaf, 1989), p. 19.

Contributors

Madhumalati Adhikari, Jabalpur

Shyam S. Agarwalla, Ram Manohar Lohia College, Ranchi

Manchi Sarat Babu, S.K. University, Anantapur

G.D. Barche, S.S.V.P.'s Arts & Commerce College

Seema Bhaduri, Bytco College, Nasik

Moutushi Chakravartee, B.T.W.R.I., Ranchi

K. Chellappan, Bharathidasan University, Tiruchi

Nila Das, University of Kalyani, West Bengal

T. Ramesh Dutta, Andhra University, Visakhapatnam

C.L.L. Jayaprada, Andhra University, Visakhapatnam

A.K. Mukherjee, B.J.B.college, Bhubaneswar

Rama Nair, Osmania University, Hyderabad

Makarand Paranjape, I.I.T., Delhi

M. Pushpa, University of Madras

M. Rajeshwar, Kakatiya University, Warangal

T. Asoka Rani, S.P. Mahila University, Tirupati

C. Visweswara Rao, S.K. University, Anantapur

Jyotsna Sahu, Utkal University, Bhubaneswar

M. Sivaramakrishna, Osmania University, Hyderabad

Ramesh K. Srivastava, G.N.D. University, Amritsar

K. Sumana, Res. Sch., S.K. University, Anantapur

Swaraj Kishen Tikoo, Manipur University, Imphal

I. Venkateswarlu, Yeshwant Mahavidyalaya, Nanded

Index